Write Your Dream Life

3 Minutes to Manifestation

Laura Di Franco

Write Your Dream Life

3 Minutes to Manifestation

Laura Di Franco

Find out more about the Write Your Dream Life Community & Manifestation Club at WriteYourDreamLife.com where we curate the energy and environment to hold each other accountable to the practice.

And for access to The Brave Healer Resource Vault, with training, masterclasses and workshops for author-entrepreneurs, go here:

https://lauradifranco.com/resources-vault/

Dedication

In honor of John F. Barnes. Without learning how to feel, none of this would've been possible. I love you.

To Dana Claudat, Esther Hicks, and Master John L. Holloway—the trifecta of masters for manifesting badassery. Thank you for your teachings and for inspiring me to be brave and not settle for anything less than my dream life.

Table of Contents

Part 2
Write to Feng Shui Your Soul

Part 3
Write to Align

Part 4
Write to Manifest
(Live in Joy)

Part 5
Write Your Dream Life Into Reality

Feathers
By Laura Di Franco

I wish I could remember
the first time I picked up
a feather—
carefully by its tip
running my thumb and forefinger
along its length
to fashion the barbs back in place

I must have been small
Mom loved the beach
Seagulls dropped
their wings everywhere
White, Black
Black and white
Shades of gray
No matter the color
to me, they shone bright gold

I remember finding my first
hawk feather
Seemed like an upgrade
Size, shape, design
My eyes wide with wonder
My awe busting through each pore
This is special
A sign from God
Better than money

Turkey feathers
Eagle feathers
Blue Jays
Cardinals
Over the years, even the tiniest
sometimes especially the tiniest
found me
I rushed over
and looked around to make sure
nobody else saw them first
Treasures, each one, for sure
Each took its place
in the many vases I curated
with these magical powers
I now possessed
A shamanic bouquet

I remember hearing my first hawk
crying above
The one that swooped in front
of my windshield
The two who beckoned me
from beyond
asking for a proper burial
These signs became
a deeper responsibility
to listen
to understand what matters.

And then in Peru
when 30 of us crossed the trails
and I happened upon
the iridescent sheen
sparkling for my eyes
and picked up that prize
looked at the sky and said,
"Thank you," quietly
because in that moment

I was more alive
than ever
and I knew. . .
. . . I knew my power.

Feathers—my magic wands
also happen to be writing utensils
The first, in fact
The very first way
we wrote actual words that
make magic
cast spells
declare laws
protect each other
make books
document the world
express love. . .
. . . what a gift, what an honor!

Nothing against hieroglyphs y'all
But these little black-and-white gems
moving themselves from heart
to pen
these poems from soul. . .
. . .these are my friends
and feathers remind me
I'm meant for them
to play
to create
to share
to be brave

Every time a feather appears
I know why I'm here
and what to do.
I'm connected
and the most important thing
I remember
is who I really am.

Introduction

I binged *Write it Down, Make it Happen* by Henriette Anne Klauser, based on a recommendation from my Feng Shui teacher, Dana. When I closed the book, I thought, *She missed a couple of things. I can't wait to write my book!*

I flashed to a book I read decades prior, *The Power of Focus*.

I've written all my goals down since I can remember! It's partly writing it, but they're missing the energy component. And nobody does the Feng Shui!

Then, I thought about how Esther Hicks teaches the Law of Attraction and getting on your high-flying disk by reaching for a better-feeling thought. I realized: *She should be adding some journaling to her homework. It's a missing piece of the puzzle.*

Enter Dana Claudat: https://www.fengshuimagical.com/

Your environment matters—the energy of it, specifically. Go ahead and think your awesome thoughts and write them all down, but if you don't curate the spaces you live in to help feed you, you're missing a component that can superpower your ability to manifest and live your dream life.

Write Your Dream Life, Three Minutes to Manifestation is about a practice of all these components of manifestation together, a power-packed combination of awareness exercises that literally helped me manifest thousands of dollars, new business collaborators, and even book awards!

Integration is the key to manifestation. This book is packed full of a lifetime of learning, lessons, and master teachings. My *why* is in the awareness practice.

If you ask me what I most wish for you, it's that you take your awareness game up a notch, body awareness, specifically. When you read this book and practice the exercises, it's the body-mind awareness practice that's going to make a life-changing difference. I wanted you to have all the various ways to do that, and I tried to think of every place or corner of your life where you could apply them.

Because, no matter what, it's the awareness that creates an opportunity for manifestation, because through your present moment awareness, you'll have a chance to notice and shift toward alignment. It's all about awareness. And this book will give you the next-level ideas and tools!

Turn the page and get started on this exciting journey of writing (and living) your dream life.

Part 1

Write for Awareness

With awareness, you have a choice.

Looking back over the decades at what brought me to this moment,
I noticed awareness gave me the choice to learn, grow, and thrive—
or stay stuck. With your awareness, what will you choose?

1.

Can You Feel?

Five years after my child reported being abused by a coach, and two years after the coach was convicted and sent to prison, I heard something that helped me wake up and feel again:

"Your anxiety can be grief."

I was in the midst of editing and publishing a book called *The Grief Experience* by lead author Kelly Daugherty and her expert cast of co-authors. The book featured chapters by therapists and coaches who've dedicated their lives to helping people navigate grief. When one of the authors uttered those words, something in me thawed.

For five years, I experienced three consequences from not feeling: anxiety and breathlessness in the form of chest tightness, intense panic, and two herniated discs. In 2023, I spent nine months mostly flat on my back, staring at the ceiling in my dining room, using a computer tray to work until my arms wore out. I got up to use the bathroom, eat, and take walks. The Universe limited me to those three activities for nine months.

You're benched, Laura. Sit and feel.

That's when I realized I was telling a five-year-old story of trauma. I kept re-telling the story in my head and to friends about my child and my part in the scenario. I ruminated heavily about every excruciating detail of the day she reported it to me, the days in court, and every day in between.

This is what happens! I thought and wrote furiously in my journal. This moment of awareness about how I was stuck in my old story was a big aha. I noticed the repetitive pattern of wanting to tell the world about what happened, how I felt, all of it. I wrote until my forearm ached. I moved the pain and the thoughts out and helped shift the story as I let that go.

I ranted to a healer friend one day about my *aha*: "This is what happens when we get stuck in our trauma story. How can I be telling the same story for five years? This isn't who I want to be. This isn't who I was born to be. I'm not a victim. With awareness, I get to choose."

One of my teachers, John F. Barnes, said, "Without awareness, we have no choice." I created my own positive version to live by:

With awareness we get a choice.

Awareness is everything, and it's the foundation of helping you write and live your dream life.

Grow Through What You Go Through, a chapter by Jennifer Thurston in *Sacred Spaces Volume 3* from Lead Author Colleen Avis, comes to mind as I share this transformation about writing my dream life. What my family and I went through is now in the past. Each of us moved through a unique healing process, and we're forever changed. Now it's time to grow—allow myself to reach for the light, sprout up from the darkness, and be who I'm meant to be from that experience. I have a choice to live, using the lessons, in any way I choose.

I'm lucky it only took five years.

Many stay paralyzed by victim mentality for the rest of their lives, letting trauma define them, missing the miracles of life sitting in front of their faces. Healing is difficult—impossible sometimes. There's no judgment. I believe we really can't fuck this up, no matter what we do.

But what if you could feel again? What if you gave yourself permission to feel everything? What would you notice? How would things change if you could anchor yourself in the present moment and notice the gifts waiting for you? What if you could embrace the pain, allow it to rise, fully feel it, and move the energy?

Laura, you've been telling the same story for five years now. Don't you think it's time to shift that to something healthier and more aligned with your vision?

Yes, wise voice. Yes, I do.

Even though I've used the pages of my journals since I was 15, it wasn't until I was 56 that something clicked, and my life shifted into high-gear manifesting mode. I took responsibility for my thoughts, words, and behaviors and dedicated myself to paying even more attention.

I shifted from writing *what is* to writing my dream life.

I shifted from using my journals to identify and honor my limiting thoughts and beliefs, complaints, pain, and trauma to a very intentional, curated practice of basking in joy, hope, peace, love, and gratitude.

With awareness, you have a choice.

But unless you allow yourself to feel (the pain, anxiety, doubt, fear, grief, terror, shame, guilt) fully and let the energy surface, release, and transform, it sits crusting over in little crevices around your heart (and other places in your body), forming energy cysts in your fascial tissue.[1] These physical-emotional-mental energy cysts create restrictions over time and begin to wreak havoc on daily function.

My 30-year career in holistic physical therapy with a focus on alternative and somato-emotional modalities prepared me to write this book. I love the science behind this. But this isn't a book just based on science.

"Words don't teach, experiences do."
~ Esther Hicks

I'm out to help you have some of those transformative experiences Esther is talking about. You can read the words here, but use your awareness and feeling, and practice the exercises so that you can embody the experiences. This will be your greatest teacher.

---

1 SEE MYOFASCIALRELEASE.COM

If you're ready to write your dream life, you'll need to give yourself permission to feel everything. You'll be ready when you're ready. I remember talking about this a lot to healer friends the year I was benched. I had enough awareness to understand I was being forced to slow down and feel. Still, I needed a little guidance because I kept getting in the way of my own process.

"I can't touch this. I need to cry, but I can't. There's a piece that's untouchable, no matter what I do. I can't access the grief. I've tried everything, literally, that I know how to do." I shared with my health coach as a lump formed in my throat. I stared at her and shifted my weight on the stool I sat on.

"Maybe it's time you stop trying and be okay with not being able to access it," said Melissa with kind eyes and a gentle voice.

"Oh, yeah. That. Okay, you're right. I'm trying too hard, and that's turning into forcing. And forcing never gets you to the release," I replied with a big sigh.

"Exactly," she said.

"Okay. That actually feels good, like a relief." I felt my shoulders drop from my ears.

"You can't fuck this up. Just let go," Melissa encouraged.

And so, I began to see the dirt I had to clean up. Seeing that dirt was the awareness I needed to take the next step.

Let's Write

For every writing exercise in this book, I encourage you to do some Brave Story Medicine™. This combines body awareness, mind awareness, and writing. So, for each "Let's Write" section, you'll practice the following awareness:

Body Awareness

- Get comfortable in your sacred writing space. Seated or lying down—your choice. There's a fantastic chapter in *Sacred Spaces* about creating your sacred writing space.

- Close your eyes, or gaze down and soften them.

- Begin taking deep breaths. Whatever kind of breathwork you enjoy is fine. The idea is to feel the breath moving in and out of your body and to use it as a feeling tool.

- Notice your breath, body, and all sensations. Practice feeling and noticing. Be curious.

- Soften your body with each exhale.

- Spend as much time here as feels good.

Thought Awareness

- As you ground and center in your body, notice your thoughts.

- Be curious, relaxed, and unattached, letting the thoughts go as you notice them.

- Notice thoughts you become attached to and return to noticing the sensation of the breath.

- Notice your thoughts, anchor into your breath, notice your thoughts, anchor into your breath.

- Soften your body with each exhale.

Writing

- Set your timer for three minutes and write as fast as you can without censoring yourself.

- As you write, pay attention to your body and notice when it clenches. Release tension as you exhale. Keep breathing. Stay connected to your body while you write.

- As you write, notice what's happening in your mind. What "voices" are moving through? Is there an argument going on? Which voice are you listening to? Which feels true? Which feels like your inner critic? Which feels like your inner wisdom? Can you tell the difference? Just notice and write it all down.

- If you begin to leave your body and land in the mess of your mind, just pause and notice what's happening. Check back in. Breathe and soften. Keep writing.

The Prompt

I feel _____. No rules; just write.

Feng Shui Activities

If I understood the full power of Feng Shui from the beginning, oh, how my life would be different today. What I'm sharing here isn't traditional Feng Shui. It's the work of The School of Intention from Dana Claudat. And the activities are shared in a very basic form. This is a huge (and phenomenal) rabbit hole I hope you explore.

Find Dana at: https://www.fengshuimagical.com/

The general principles:

1. Declutter

2. Clean

3. Clear

4. Curate

The following activities throughout the book might be for your physical spaces or for the vessel you inhabit (your body-mind-soul). Either way, we declutter, clean, clear, and curate those spaces to create the purest channels for energy flow and manifestation possible.

Couple your writing with Feng Shui and positive thinking, and you'll feel your superpowers come alive.

Feng Shui Home Survey

Do a home survey:

Grab your notebook and pen and take a tour of every room and space of your home. Note what needs attention. What needs to be decluttered, fixed, repaired, painted, or redecorated? Notice what brings you joy, and what doesn't. If it's not lighting you up with joy, why do you have it around you?

Write a list for each room you can begin tackling. "See the dirt" in your spaces and make a plan to declutter, clean, clear, and curate.

If you'd like to start on the list, choose the smallest project first—maybe a drawer, your wallet, or a closet—and begin the decluttering process.

Work your way through every space of your home and declutter.

Once your spaces are decluttered, clean them with healthy, natural cleaning products you love.

Next, we'll work on seeing more of the dirt.

Room to write. . .

2.

To Clean House, You Must First See the Dirt

"If you want to clean house, you must first see the dirt."
~ Louise Hay

Writing to gain awareness is a powerful healing tool. Feeling is healing. When we write to feel, we write to heal. You're not going to leap from pain to purpose and passion without feeling. If you try to skip feeling and healing, you'll write your dream life on top of a huge, messy pile of shit. Don't let that messy pile of shit be your life's foundation. You can't build on it. It just smears on the sidewalk.

What you can do is transform it into things like strength and resilience. But not by forcing it. Being aware of the dirt gives you a chance to clean it up. Being aware of the thoughts and beliefs you hold about your life gives you a chance to be curious, ask questions, and change, which can change your whole life.

"Seeing the dirt" is a requirement for writing your dream life because what you can't see, you can't clean. When thoughts and beliefs you aren't aware of run your life, you have no choice but to live your life by those rules. You'll stay stuck. What else is possible?

This noticing and cleaning of your thoughts and feelings is one step in the Feng Shui of your internal environment (more on that in Part 2). I've been seeing the dirt in my journals since I was 15. Yikes. That's a lot of focus on the dirt. You can move through it faster than I did.

When I became an adult and started working through my thoughts and limiting beliefs, I noticed there were some intense themes running my life.

I was limited by repeating thoughts like:

You're too stupid to make this work.
Nobody likes you.
You're not pretty enough.

I used my journals, read what I wrote, and in some instances pulled back from the page and said out loud, "Whoa, do I actually think that?" It was time to see and clean up the dirt!

Now it's your turn to see the dirt.

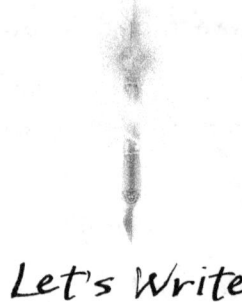

Let's Write

Remember to do your body and mind awareness practice (even if it's three breaths' worth) before you write. Set your timer for three minutes and write as fast as you can without censoring yourself. If three minutes isn't enough, give yourself as much time as needed and write until you're complete. You'll often notice a natural pause where the writing slows and finishes.

The Prompt

Make a list of any limiting beliefs or repeated thoughts that are self-sabotaging in nature. When they're "out loud" (on the paper), you can use that as an awareness tool.

Room to write. . .

_____

_____

_____

_____

_____

_____

_____

_____

_____

_____

_____

_____

_____

_____

_____

_____

_____

_____

_____

_____

_____

_____

Feng Shui

Choose one space in your home where you spend the most time. This could easily be your bedroom, since we spend on average one-third of our lives sleeping. But you could also choose your workspace, art space, or kitchen.

After completing the decluttering and cleaning in that space, use an energy-clearing process you love. Any clearing activity you choose will shift stagnant energy and open up your space to more flow. This is a process that bears repeating to keep your spaces in the best possible energy flow.

Examples of space clearing activities:

- Smudge the space (Palo Santo is my fave)

- Clap in the corners of the room

- Use a singing bowl

- Place bowls of salt around the room (or explore salt burning)

For more space-clearing techniques, see Dana's YouTube channel: https://www.youtube.com/@thetaoofdana

In the next chapter, we'll get to the core of opening up your mindset to write your dream life: worthiness.

3.

Worthiness

"I realize my whole life has been a pursuit of reclaiming my worth. Every single thing I want for my life points back to how unworthiness has been in the way of it," Beth told me.

My conversation with a healer friend was deep that day, and it all circled back to worthiness. I instantly resonated with what she said and nodded.

"Yes, for many people it really comes down to this, to feeling worthy. So many of us experienced a childhood that created the belief that our worth was related to being or doing the right thing, being a good girl," I replied with a mental flash to a childhood scene that created a little bit of tightness in my chest.

"Our parents did the best they could with what they had," said Beth with a tone of gentle understanding and forgiveness.

"Yes, they did, but you know that Maya Angelou quote, right?"

"When you know better, you do better."

"Yeah," I replied, smiling. The bigness of our topic was hitting me and I looked up like I often do when I feel like the Universe is speaking through my friends.

"I feel like my healing journey has been for the entire ancestral line," Beth continued.

"Yes! Exactly. What we're doing now will help the generations behind and after us. We're doing the healing they couldn't do!" I exclaimed, sitting up a little straighter as I spoke.

"This worthiness thing is rough. It seems so ingrained, so difficult to heal. I get triggered so easily into that little girl who isn't enough," said Beth.

"With awareness. . ."

"We get a choice!"

Beth and I laughed as we continued our conversation about healing unworthiness.

You were born, so you're worthy. Why it took a lifetime for that to sink in is a tough question. Divine timing and all, right?

Over the decades of my studies, talking to healers, getting guidance, journaling, and practicing noticing my thoughts of unworthiness, I started to make some space and observe the trigger. Making that space was crucial, a key to slowing down the triggers. This truth of feeling worthy is something we come to in so many unique ways. It took hearing it many times before I shifted my triggered reactions into slower responses and began to step into my power.

Reclaiming your worth is a step toward empowerment. It's a beautiful step we all need to take to live the life we dream of. How will you begin to create your own shift?

As you allow the truth of your worth sink in today, feel it, embody it, and allow it to drive your life. What would it look like to walk through your life knowing your worth and setting boundaries to protect it?

Setting boundaries based on your foundational feeling of worth, values, and desires, well, we'll need a whole other book for that. For now, begin to reflect on what that means for you. What are the sacred boundaries you'll begin to enforce based on your feeling of total worthiness?

That fear of unworthiness, of not being good enough—that impostor syndrome—it's boring. What else is possible today?

In the most empowered version of you, what would you say, do, be?

There's a little bit of dirt left in the form of unworthiness; it's time to clean and clear that out. Only, you can't analyze your way there. Allow the feelings to rise and be felt, and transform that energy.

Let's Write

Remember to do your body and mind awareness practice (even if it's three breaths' worth) before you write. Set your timer for three minutes and write as fast as you can without censoring yourself. If three minutes isn't enough, give yourself as much time as needed and write until you're complete. You'll often notice a natural pause where the writing slows and finishes.

The Prompt

If there were nobody left to offend, upset, or disappoint, I would _____.

Room to write. . .

Feng Shui

Are there things in your spaces that you don't like, are broken (stained, cracked, torn, missing pieces, etc.), or that you own because someone else bought them, but they're not your style?

Declutter them from your environment.

In my case, I sent a large load to Goodwill that included furniture my ex acquired, art I no longer enjoyed, and clothes I hadn't worn in a couple of years.

Begin to make space for what brings you joy, love, confidence, and courage. Begin to make space for what helps you feel empowered by discarding items (and old, unhelpful beliefs) that don't.

Next, we'll explore the negativity bias and how to transform that.

4.

Negativity and Victim Consciousness

There's nothing like a really great excuse to stay in victim consciousness. How can we blame victims of trauma and tragedy for this? They have the ultimate reason for the way they are, how they think, and their inability to trust again: Victim consciousness feels like the truth. It's their truth, and they own it. And this isn't a place for an entire psychological analysis of healing from trauma. But it is a place to become aware of patterns and understand the possibility of changing them.

I know for sure I was groomed by my daughter's abuser, which eventually allowed this person access to her. Thinking about all of the details of this scene brings me back into anger, frustration (I'm clenching my teeth as I write this), and the ultimate belief that I could've done something to prevent what happened. *This was my fault* was a belief I held for a really long time.

"I am this thing that happened to me" is part of what I started noticing. I created an identity around an event, and who I was because of it, and then attached to that as who I was.

I recognized the self-sabotage and began to understand other ways to think about the scenario. I recognized the attachment to the story and began to create new ways to be in the world that had nothing to do with that event.

Realizing I told the same story for five years woke me up to my responsibility to do something about the pattern I recognized in myself. Realizing it's our journey to take responsibility for everything that's happened in our lives (and our future) feels overwhelming. For me, that's the ultimate freedom.

Now one of my mantras is: I *get* to take responsibility for my life—every single piece of it. Nobody has control over my awareness and my responses to what's happening. Only I get to choose how I respond.

"Nobody is going to do this for you."

You've heard this before, but what does it mean to you?

What it takes to move from victim mentality to embracing responsibility is a whole lotta awareness and willingness to be and feel vulnerable. It's a willingness to go for "happy" instead of "right." It's a journey to choosing thoughts and beliefs that are about the joy you prefer to feel.

What is the moment that switched a lightbulb on for you? Did you reach out to get help? Did you begin to take responsibility in any way you could and make steps (even baby steps) toward transformation?

Now, lets say you're getting your own awareness game on and it's going well, but then you have to go out into the big bad world and actually talk to other humans. That's tough some days, especially when it feels like the world and everyone in it is in doomsday mindset.

We have the power to choose change, but some never do. Free will, right?

We all know negative people. We see the victim loop they're stuck in. In fact, it's always easier to see where someone else is stuck than to see our own stuck places, isn't it?

They have great excuses for being stuck. And some of us try so hard to show them their ways, knowing very well we can't do anything to wake them up. Only they can do that. However, we can be great role models. We can allow them to experience us—our thoughts, our behaviors, the ways we show up in the world, our brave words and actions. We can model courage.

And what can you model for your badass self? Are you being your own best role model? What opportunities for healing can you identify? Are you staying true to what you say you want for your dream life? What old stories are you stuck in? What's your new focus? What did you learn? What opportunity did you (or do you) have to heal?

Your awareness will help you see where huge opportunities for transformation exist.

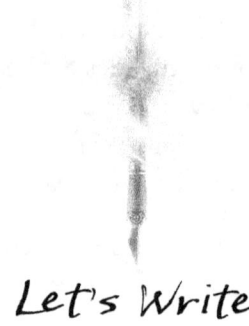

Let's Write

Let's observe and clear a bit more dirt here.

Remember to do your body and mind awareness practice (even if it's three breaths' worth) before you write. Set your timer for three minutes and write as fast as you can without censoring yourself. If three minutes isn't enough, give yourself as much time as needed and write until you're complete. You'll often notice a natural pause where the writing slows and finishes.

The Prompt

The old story I've been telling myself is _____.

Begin to call out any leftover negativity or negative bias you have about any subjects in your life. Often, they're the things we know we're right about.

What do you know you're right about? Would you rather be right, or would you rather be happy?

Recognizing is the miracle step one to everything great that comes after it. Because without awareness, you'll remain stuck, unconscious, and in the old bad habits.

Room to write. . .

_____

_____

_____

_____

_____

_____

_____

_____

_____

_____

_____

_____

_____

_____

_____

_____

_____

_____

_____

_____

_____

Feng Shui

Your spaces also tell (possible old) stories. Look around, especially in the spaces where you create or spend the most time. What story is that space telling? Does it activate the "victim loop" you're working to rewire? Is it dark, dirty, dusty, or ignored? Or is it bright, spacious, and enjoyable? How does your space make you feel when you enter it?

What's the new story you want your space to tell? Begin by making a few notes about what you want to change, and make a plan!

After my divorce, the story I saw everywhere was my inability to speak up about the things I felt and wanted for my life. Everything in my home was brown, literally. One of the first rooms I painted was my red room—a tribute to and altar for bold, brave badassery.

Let's take this a step further now and talk more about your past stories.

5.

Stories of the Past

Our identity is woven into our past and its stories. Everything that has happened in my past has created a path that led me here, so I believe in gratitude for all of it. Who am I if that thing didn't happen to me?

When past regret muddies my now-moment and future dreams, my ability to co-create my life with Source—my momentum, as Esther Hicks calls it—slows way down.

Every thought against what you desire slows your roll. Every single one. It bogs down the momentum of creation and manifestation. And if you're like me, and your brain runs a million miles a minute, it feels so difficult to believe you'll ever have control over it.

But even with my million-mile-a-minute mind, I adopted a practice that gained momentum. And it helps to shift the stories of the past. Whenever your mind is on the past, you dabble with regret, sadness, and sometimes depression. Sad moments from the past, or stories about the person you were before this moment, don't offer opportunities to create what you want moving forward.

We do this a lot, and it's such a potent thought pattern that we sometimes fall unconscious under its spell.

Your feelings about who you were before—the scenes and stories from your past life—don't help you feel good in the now.

I have compassion for little Laura. Some of the old stories are easy to shift. I have less compassion for 20-something Laura because when I think back on some moments in her life, I cringe. *Girl, what the hell were you thinking?*

I've learned to go easy on now-Laura when she's flooded with those memories. I had a little EMDR for some of that (really powerful therapy for healing old shit).

I go easier on now-Laura when she starts to tell stories about her 30s and 40s. I easily find myself shifting or pivoting from those feelings and moving toward something that feels better. The evolution of awareness is like a movie over the decades, and it has gotten better. She has learned so many lessons.

But even in the recent past (the last five years), trauma occurred that triggered me into all my old stories of unworthiness.

Can you be gentler with yourself?

It's a question I ask myself more often now. The now-Laura needs a gentle approach. Self-forgiveness is an enormous task when we think of past stories. *I did the best I could with the awareness I had then.*

It's like thinking about anybody who treated you poorly in the past and coming to forgiveness. You understand that they were also doing the best they could with the upbringing, information, resources, or capacity they had at the time. We're not condoning behavior; we're being gentler in the name of the now-moment where we'd like to manifest our dream life.

It's important to embrace this kind of awareness daily. Only with this kind of awareness do you get the choice to hit the pause button in the middle of telling (or identifying with) a past story and choose something more helpful.

Recognizing the power of being aware of those past story moments is huge.

This is a powerful practice of noticing the thoughts in your head. And, as I've repeated (purposefully), it's all about awareness. This is the huge gift we get, the opportunity to recognize that it's all in our control. Because our awareness is the one thing that's up to us in every single moment.

Let's Write

Remember to do your body and mind awareness practice (even if it's three breaths' worth) before you write. Set your timer for three minutes and write as fast as you can without censoring yourself. If three minutes isn't enough, give yourself as much time as needed and write until you're complete. You'll often notice a natural pause where the writing slows and finishes.

The Prompt

The great thing about my past is _____.

If you get stuck on this prompt because your past has been very difficult, I challenge you to pause, breathe, and look for the moments in that difficult past when you discovered your resilience or what you were made of. Allow yourself to receive that moment of clarity about how the past story got you to the now, and what gift of learning was there for you.

Room to write. . .

_____

_____

_____

_____

_____

_____

_____

_____

_____

_____

_____

_____

_____

_____

_____

_____

_____

_____

_____

_____

_____

Feng Shui

What moments from your past are visible in your space? How do they make you feel? Are you holding onto old objects, paint colors, furniture, or other ways and habits in your daily life that are just that: habits? Are you holding on out of obligation, or not wanting to upset someone else?

Make a few notes about the objects, thoughts, beliefs, traditions, or behaviors you'll keep because they bring you joy—or that you'll shift because they don't.

I hung onto a filing cabinet full of old school papers, report cards, and ripped construction paper art because they were moments from my kids' past. The reality was, they cluttered my space. When I opened those spaces, not only was my filing cabinet free to file important papers I needed to access, but every time I opened a drawer, I could take a deeper breath.

Decluttering old stories (and objects) creates space. Where there's space, new energy can flow. Where new energy flows, there's healing.

Now, what about future worries? Let's get to it.

6.

Worry About the Future

I'm guilty of this version of self-sabotage more often than others. Worrying about the future triggers a deep, relentless ache. It sneaks unannounced into my otherwise fantastic day.

Many times, this worry rides in on a "hit" from earlier that day: something that was said or something bad that happened. One bad thing leads to lots of bad thoughts, and sooner or later, I'm feeling pretty down.

What if it's not enough?
What if I'm not enough?
What if I fail?
What if it all goes away?
What if. . .

I've watched this pattern happen numerous times. I have a level of awareness that helps me shift it. If it's future worry, I notice, pause, recognize what I'm creating with my worry, and then shift to a present-moment body awareness, a little stillness meditation, or just notice the gorgeous birds on the feeder outside. Right now is the generous present moment that will solve your future worry in a few seconds if you practice pressing the pause button.

What do you notice in yourself when it comes to future thinking, worry, and anxiety? When your thoughts are in the future, anxiety typically becomes your companion.

Of course, there are positive versions of past and future thinking. You may have a past story of accomplishment or joy. You may have a future plan that excites you. But when I think of past or future positives, they never hold the safety or power of my present moment, or the present opportunity I have to create a high-vibe feeling. All the control you'll ever have in life is in the response to your now-present moment.

Notice the chapter title says "Worry." You can dream and imagine a positive future that hasn't happened yet and practice its vibes. But if you're practicing future worry, please pause that train and regroup.

The generous present moment can anchor you in joy; just use your senses. What do you hear? What do you smell? Close your eyes and listen. That one action will ground you in the now, much better than the spiral of worry that was taking you down.

I love a passage in Dr. Wayne Dyer's book *Excuses Begone* that goes like this: "If you're not 100% sure of a future outcome, whether it will turn out positive or negative, the best thing to do while you wait is to imagine the positive outcome. It does no good to ruminate on the worst-case scenario."

And then there's the quote: "Worrying is like praying for the bad thing to happen."

Why do we do this to ourselves? Breathe. Come back to the present. Anchor into your senses. Still your mind. And then use your writing to shift that energy and create something more helpful, healthier, or more aligned.

Let's Write

Remember to do your body and mind awareness practice (even if it's three breaths' worth) before you write. Set your timer for three minutes and write as fast as you can without censoring yourself. If three minutes isn't enough, give yourself as much time as needed and write until you're complete. You'll often notice a natural pause where the writing slows and finishes.

The Prompt

Right now, in this generous present moment, I am powerful and I can feel
_____.

Room to write. . .

Feng Shui

Feng Shui opens up space for your future to flow in and arrive. So, now that you've been decluttering a bit and starting to clean and clear spaces (both internal and external), what kinds of new dreams can you create in this very moment?

Is there a space in your home where you love to write, dream, meditate, or do yoga? Begin to imagine (or create) a sacred space you'll enjoy being in regularly, even if it's one corner of a room.

My dining room became this space for me. It has a large, sliding glass door that catches the afternoon sunlight, so my suncatchers beam rainbows all over the walls every day. I love writing and dreaming in that room.

Let's move through some examples of doing the work of healing when life gets in the way of our high vibes. Grief is something we'll all go through, one way or another—and we can still write our dream life in the midst of it.

7.

Grief and Anxiety

"I'm feeling the panic in my chest. It builds and becomes almost unbearable. Is this a panic attack? I've never had one of those before, but this feels like what people describe."

Melissa, my health coach, was gentle (as always) with her answer. "What was going on that may have triggered it?"

"I'm not sure. They seem to happen for no reason at all. Sometimes they happen at night, and the feeling wakes me up, like I'm having a bad dream." I tried to explain it and realized I couldn't. I just kept rubbing my chest with my palm while I talked.

It was during this time that one of the authors from *The Grief Experience* said, "Your anxiety can be grief."

That one line resonated so deeply. After our multiple-year, intense family trauma, I was left with physical symptoms and no real reason for them, except the obvious. So, when it clicked for me that my building anxiety could be grief, I felt a huge inhale rise up through my chest and ribs— and an even bigger exhale of healing, letting go, and acknowledgement. Sometimes one line can change your life.

When you're in the game to manifest your best life, you're most often also dealing with some level of trauma and grief, small, medium, or large. You can't really live life unscathed, unless you're a monk on a mountaintop and don't have access to the civilized world. But then it's about other kinds of trauma, isn't it?

So, what can you do with grief and anxiety when they're a reality of life, and you know ignoring, stuffing, or otherwise bypassing the feelings isn't healthy?

I use a feeling-shift combo here when I tap into trauma feelings or triggers that surface. I like to honor the feeling by giving myself permission to feel it fully, use my awareness to pause my mind and clear anything I'm making the feeling mean, and then allow the release to move through at its own pace.

I'm reading the last paragraph with a little chuckle. This isn't easy at the beginning of the journey, when you're triggered and reactive—and maybe say something you don't mean to the people closest to you. With time and practice, moving through grief and anxiety with grace and ease is possible. It takes a keen awareness and a commitment to that awareness to become a master at the shift. It's worth the practice and work.

At one point recently, the feeling of anxiety brewing in my chest became so uncomfortable, I had to get up from my bed (where I happily slept moments before) and move. I was forced to move my body to shift the feeling. It shifted quickly. I was relieved and went back to sleep.

The next time it happened, I decided to stay with the feeling without moving—to honor it and its intensity with my breath. I followed Melissa's instructions: "Breathe through each breath easily and gently. Don't strain. Pay attention to the sensation of the breath as it moves through you and the feeling you're having."

After several minutes of lying there, not moving, just breathing, the feeling shifted gently, and it felt organic. The shift felt more complete. It felt like healing.

I was happy to discern the difference between the feeling and the action I took to change it—and something I did that helped the feeling change in its own time.

Can you feel the difference between those two?

Awareness is everything. Discernment is next-level awareness. With discernment, I can begin to shift and write my life.

Let's Write

Remember to do your body and mind awareness practice (even if it's three breaths' worth) before you write. Set your timer for three minutes and write as fast as you can without censoring yourself. If three minutes isn't enough, give yourself as much time as needed and write until you're complete. You'll often notice a natural pause where the writing slows and finishes.

The Prompt

I'm able to breathe through any feeling with grace and ease, and I love the way I can _____.

And one more to try:

Being able to feel is a gift that's given me _____.

Room to write. . .

Feng Shui

"You can grieve joyfully," said Dana, and I had a lightbulb moment about the straitjacket I wore around my heart. I put it there, of course.

In the world of Feng Shui, space to breathe and dream is everything. The energy of that space is everything. I felt a shift with the statement and realized if I paid attention to my inner environment, I could release the bracing with one deep breath and make space around my heart.

Is there anything you're grieving right now? Most of us experience some level of grief at any given time. Check in with your body to notice how it's holding everything together. Where is there tightening, clamping down, or bracing? Do you notice muscles clenching?

Sometimes you have to clench tighter, then release, to realize the amount of clenching you did to begin with. This clenching can become an unconscious holding pattern. Those patterns can lead to pain and dysfunction.

Full-Body Release:

1. Start with your face, scrunching it up with your furrowed brow and tight jaw—one, two, three… then release on an exhale.

2. Next, the shoulders: Raise them up to the sky—one, two, three. . . then release on an exhale.

3. Bend your elbows, doing a bicep curl while clenching your fists tight—one, two, three. . .then release on an exhale.

4. Tighten your stomach, holding your breath—one, two, three. . . then release with a sigh on the exhale.

5. Clench your butt and thigh muscles—one, two, three. . .then release on the next exhale.

6. Tighten your whole body at once—one, two, three. . .and release in one big, softening exhale. Make space around your heart for it to plump and beat a little bigger.

When you're in your body and noticing its patterns, that awareness gives you a choice, and that's powerful. Your body messages will let you know for sure. Let's talk about that next.

8.

What You Know for Sure

I saw this chapter title in my outline and felt a surge of excitement. *This might be the awareness that's changed my life the most: questioning everything I think I know for sure.*

Whether it was with my ex, a client with a complaint, or something a friend or family member said that felt upsetting, I wanted desperately to be right and had to pause. I had to get and feel vulnerable. I remember too many instances to pick one for you, unfortunately. And they still happen, all the time. Only now, I'm quicker to pause, quicker to apologize, and much quicker to realize that what I know for sure is only based on my own lived experience.

What you know for sure, believe without a doubt, and especially know you're right about are the exact things to examine when you desire to change your life.

For those connected to your intuition at another level, I want you to focus on what you know is right (not what you know for sure). It's a small difference, but important. Take your knowing and examine it. What parts of your knowing are that bigger intuitive connection, and what parts have a slightly off, "old belief" feeling?

Understanding what you know is right and being willing to examine those things is a game-changer.

I have beliefs that are old, ingrained, and create a sort of stubborn unwillingness to listen. I've noticed this in my body. I've figured out when it comes up in me and taught myself to pause to give myself a chance to either change or stick with my belief.

The simple pause and willingness to examine a belief you've held for a really long time is already a ninja move. Sitting with that feeling of rightness and questioning whether it's healthy, aligned, or possibly holding you back from transformation is so powerful. Your power lies in both the willingness and the ability to practice feeling vulnerable.

Maybe I'm not right about this.

Maybe there's another way to think about this.

Maybe, just maybe, I've held myself back because I wasn't willing to bend about this topic.

There's one caveat here. Most of the experienced healers I know—the ones who walk in awareness every day—are used to examining their thoughts and beliefs. They're curious. They question their thoughts, beliefs, and behaviors. Understanding the opportunity, they can actually go too far and sabotage themselves.

Questioning their own beliefs by default leads to uncertainty or lack of clarity in their pursuit of more awareness. They don't know when to fully trust themselves, set boundaries, or stand up for what they know or know is right for them in the moment.

The awareness of questioning what I think I know for sure has changed my life. But so has the awareness of what it feels like to know my truth in the moment and resist over-analyzing it.

It's a balance, and your present-moment awareness will be the answer to figuring it out.

What I'd like you to ponder is the feeling of "knowing" in your body. Now would be a great time to write down all the ways you'd describe that.

Let's Write

Remember to do your body and mind awareness practice (even if it's three breaths' worth) before you write. Set your timer for three minutes and write as fast as you can without censoring yourself. If three minutes isn't enough, give yourself as much time as needed and write until you're complete. You'll often notice a natural pause where the writing slows and finishes.

The Prompt

Describe all the ways your body feels when you know something is right or good for you. If you're still fine-tuning this practice, you might just sit and imagine something you love and notice what you feel in your body as you do that.

Examples: Warm, tingly, free, easy, light. . .

Room to write. . .

Feng Shui

When I realized Feng Shui could apply to my body, I had a big *aha* about what I was doing to clear this sacred vessel and make it an open channel for high-vibe energy.

Divine messages flow, when I take care of my body and keep it energetically "clean," but it gets even better than that. My clair senses are enhanced. I know stuff. I know stuff before it happens. And I manifest like a badass.

So, what are you doing to keep your body vessel clean and clear today?

Here's a short list of ways to energetically clear your body. See which ones resonate and choose something to try:

1. A bath or shower (yes, that simple). It's why some people like to bathe at night, to clear the energy of the day before they climb into bed.

2. Eating only whole foods for a day (or more). Depending on your nutrition and eating habits, this may be more complicated. But being aware that food is not only nourishment, but also medicine is important. Every bite is energy your body uses to keep you healthy.

3. Breathwork. Any length of time is great. It's a powerful modality that will wash you from the inside out.

4. Getting sunlight and fresh air. Do some earthing by getting barefoot on the grass or sand, preferably in the sunlight. It's a powerful nervous system reset.

5. Take a day off all screens and artificial light. Let your body sink back into its natural rhythms.

I could list 100 things here. The biggest question: How are you taking care of your body and practicing the Feng Shui it deserves?

One way we move stagnant energy is through forgiveness. It's a powerful healing tool that creates space for higher vibes.

9.

Forgiveness

Awareness around forgiveness can be profoundly healing. When you're writing your dream life, and you have forgiveness work to do, it's important to slow down and try to complete as much of this work as you can.

In my life, I've mostly tried to forgive myself for the things I've said and done that I'm either not proud of or, worse, humiliated by. My self-love (see next chapter) is the practice, and it starts with me before I can move to others.

So far, that work has been ongoing and lifelong as an aware adult. Maybe if we accept that we'll never get it all done, we can breathe and release in this precious moment. What I know about this sometimes very difficult work is every nugget of release helps clear a path, change the energy in me, and opens sacred space for healing.

"How do you forgive someone who has hurt you, or someone you love?" I asked in another conversation shortly after our family trauma.

"Everyone has to be included when we talk about healing. Everyone. Even perpetrators," my wise friend Jean replied.

"I find myself very protective of those kinds of thoughts," I pushed back. "People want to burn the perpetrators at the stake. They're unable to wrap their minds around the idea that everyone, even the worst of us, needs (deserves) healing. I know healing isn't reserved for only some people. In my case, this must make me the worst mom ever."

I looked down and noticed I gripped one hand with the other and felt my body tense up. *How will I ever talk about this with normal people?*

"This is tricky, for sure," Jean said. "But you're not a bad mom. On the contrary, you are the change."

Jean's reassurance helped, but I still wasn't sure internally. *I'm not sure how I will share this topic with my audience.*

Once upon a time, I had a really awesome business mentor who put this another way: "Bless those who did you wrong and send them on their way with those blessings."

Her point was that the giver of blessings is in blessing energy, and that's what you need for manifestation. I've thought about this for other feelings such as guilt, frustration, and anger. Those energies can feel like poison. How can we stop poisoning ourselves?

I used that advice in the middle of my divorce year when conversations got heated and impossible. Remember what Dr. Phil always reminded us? "Would you rather be right, or would you rather be happy?"

**In the quest to write a dream life,
the answer is always about being happy.**

If you want to be in manifesting mode, you must always peek at the moments that trigger you the most, the ones you know you're right about, and choose happiness instead.

Even though that conversation (and many of them to follow) was difficult, and I felt like we were going in circles, I finished with an intentional prayer:

I wish him the best and send high-vibe healing energy to him now and always.

It takes a badass to bless someone who pisses you off, says hurtful things, or worse, physically/mentally/emotionally harms you or someone you love. But forgiveness and manifestation get you to a point where you realize you're not forgiving them; you're shifting your energy and focus for *you.*

Who do you need to forgive? Do you need to forgive yourself, too?

I read an amazing book called *Radical Forgiveness* by Colin Tipping that uses letter writing as a tool. Check it out.

Let's Write

Remember to do your body and mind awareness practice (even if it's three breaths' worth) before you write. Set your timer for three minutes and write as fast as you can without censoring yourself. If three minutes isn't enough, give yourself as much time as needed and write until you're complete. You'll often notice a natural pause where the writing slows and finishes.

The Prompt

I forgive _____ for _____.

After you journal, there's always a wonderful opportunity to pause and reflect on how you feel as a result of moving thoughts, beliefs, and ideas from your head/body to the page. Take a moment (as many as you need) to reflect, breathe, and maybe even write more.

Room to write. . .

_____

_____

_____

_____

_____

_____

_____

_____

_____

_____

_____

_____

_____

_____

_____

_____

_____

_____

_____

_____

_____

Feng Shui

This Feng Shui practice also happens to be a writing practice. Choose someone (or yourself) to write a letter of forgiveness to. You can send this letter, or if the person is deceased, you can create a burning ritual after you write it to release the energy. This ritual can also apply to living people with whom you have no contact.

Who will you write your letter of forgiveness to?

A true release in full forgiveness is a powerful, energetic force you will feel inside, typically helping you feel lighter and happier.

10.

Self-Love

My golden nuggets about self-love came slowly but surely over a decade, once I prioritized my own health, wellness, and desires over everyone else's. Many people share a story of doing everything for everyone else for decades before having the *aha* that they haven't lived their own lives. I'm one of those people.

Many days, it felt safer to follow the shoulds and supposed-tos I learned along the way. That seemed low-risk until melancholy accumulated and stuck in my throat more often than not. I began to question everything— like, every single moment that brought me to that one.

I'd love to tell you the self-love poured in, and I behaved differently right away, but it didn't. It took years and many moments, building upon each other, to find a way of being that put my health and wellness first so that I could serve others. That included my kids, which many parents will tell you is why they prioritize others over themselves.

There's a way to put yourself first and serve in the ways you must. The trick is to find your way.

Oxygen mask? Yes, and. . .

. . .why doesn't this really hit home for people? Maybe because it's dumbed down for a family audience.

How about this: You will die if you don't put that mask on yourself first. And then, the people counting on you might also die.

Taking this back a notch, think about burnout. Your workaholic tendencies (good intentions or not) are like ignoring the oxygen mask. You will burn out, get sick, and land in the hospital if you can't understand that self-love and care *must* come to you first.

People doing this success thing with power and impact strategically employ radical self-love and self-care.

We don't celebrate radical self-love and self-care often enough. In fact, people around you may be sabotaging your efforts. Don't let them. The biggest lesson I've learned is to stop saying yes out of FOMO (fear of missing out) and only say yes when the invitation is fully aligned with my life or business goals. Many people may be asking you to show up or do things. It doesn't mean you have to say yes to all of them.

You loving and caring for yourself often means having to say no to people, places, and events, or even canceling prior commitments.

Your promise of integrity gets in the way of beginning this journey. You say yes (and keep your promises) and burn out, instead of standing up for your own health and canceling. We've been taught it's what we're supposed to do to be "good" and "professional," or whatever other word triggers you so badly you're willing to sabotage your own health to maintain the optics.

"It's the optics of it."

Those five words from my ex infuriated me. There are people in your life that will be so concerned about what others around them think that they allow that to drive their behavior. This will eventually backfire.

"I don't give a fuck about optics. We're talking about mental health, here!" I replied, feeling the heat rise in my cheeks.

When you get to the point where what everyone else thinks about you comes second to what you know you need to be healthy, you win.

I'm winning this self-love and self-care game, finally. And when you get ahead in this game, you really can't go back. Everything moving forward is about more love and care. And that's some high-vibe badassery that will help you write a dream life!

One last story about simple self-care. I had to love myself enough to get back to a work schedule that a human could endure. I reached robot levels (and peak awareness) when I reached over to my phone (that buzzed and woke me up) one night, picked it up and started to type a response to an acquaintance who had a question about a program I run.

What are you doing? Go back to sleep. They can wait until morning!

Now, I'm asking you, dear reader, how will you regulate your nervous system and ground and center yourself in manifesting energy if you train yourself to respond to every stimuli like a robot? It's not sustainable. Let the rest of the world spin up into a frenzy, while you understand the solution—pause, breathe, sleep, and take radical care of yourself. You will be the one left standing to change the world.

Let's Write

Remember to do your body and mind awareness practice (even if it's three breaths' worth) before you write. Set your timer for three minutes and write as fast as you can without censoring yourself. If three minutes isn't enough, give yourself as much time as needed and write until you're complete. You'll often notice a natural pause where the writing slows and finishes.

The Prompt

I love you, (insert your first name). You are _____ (write all the things you love about yourself, including your strengths, personality traits, accomplishments, physical and mental features, etc.).

Room to write. . .

Feng Shui

When I started to create spaces based on what I love, my whole house transformed. Your entire house is a major Feng Shui project, and you can tackle it room by room.

Today, pick a small space you spend a lot of time in and clear the countertops, desktops, or other table/dresser tops. The stovetop is a space to pay particular attention to.

Clearing space like this might sound simple, but it's so powerful.

First, declutter, then clean with your favorite natural cleaning products. Then, decide what will go back onto the counters, being careful not to clutter them up again.

You're making more sacred space to create, to cook, to write and paint, and to love yourself!

If you don't own the book *The Life-Changing Power of Self-Love* by lead author Tina Green, I hope you'll pick it up. You'll own an incredible expert toolkit for this topic. Sometimes, we need to read the story or practice the tool that's written for us before the puzzle piece clicks into place, and that aha feeling settles into our bones. With so many stories and self-love strategies in that book, you'll find the one that was written for you.

Now that we've begun this journey with the most foundational component—awareness—we can continue with using writing itself as a clearing process. In Part 2, writing will be the prompt and the Feng Shui practice.

Part 2

Write to Feng Shui Your Soul

Since I was 15 years old, the blank pages of my journals have been a sacred space to declutter, clean, and clear (to Feng Shui) my thoughts and inner world. The sacred act of putting your pen to paper—of moving your ideas from heart to pen to paper—is the process and practice of writing to Feng Shui your soul. Writing is a powerful awareness practice. In this section of the book, the writing *is* the Feng Shui!

11.

Your Sacred Writing Space

*[The following excerpt is from the book **Sacred Spaces** by lead author Colleen Avis. I wrote Chapter 24, "Feng Shui Your Soul First, How to Set Up Your Sacred Writing Space."]*

How to Set Up Your Sacred Writing Space

First of all, know this matters. Every space you live in matters. So, if you're motivated after this chapter, go discover the information awaiting you. The rabbit hole on this one is real but powerful. Learn more about Feng Shui and decluttering strategies. Start small. Baby steps are better than no steps. Hence, starting you off with your writing space.

My friend Dana Claudat: https://www.fengshuimagical.com/ has incredible resources for you. Then, when you're ready to publish your brave words for the world to read, I'm your gal.

What you need:

- A notebook and pen to write down what you see, feel, and want to change in your writing space.

- A non-toxic cleaner and rag for the dust.

- A recycling bin for the paper.

- A trash can for the junk.

- Your favorite essential oils, objects, notebooks, candles, etc., to adorn your new space with.

1. Survey your writing space. Where do you write and create? Do you have a dedicated, sacred space for this? If not, why not? If literal space is an issue, think about a sacred corner of a room where you can set up a small desk and chair. Decide on where your space is going to be.

2. Assess your seating. Your desk or table and chair should be comfortable and ergonomically set up so your body is supported and relaxed. Increased tension in your shoulders, arms, back, and neck will shorten your ability to be in the flow. The physical therapist in me wants you to compare the sitting posture for writing to a yoga pose. It's a therapeutic position that can enhance or hurt you. Make it a good one.

3. Assess your lighting. Great lighting is both an eyesight and an energy thing. How's the lighting in your writing space? Is there natural light? How can you increase that? Do lightbulbs need dusting off or changing? How about the light fixtures or lamps themselves? Clean it all and arrange better lighting for your workspace. Add candles and Himalayan salt lamps for extra magical juju.

4. Clean your desktop. I didn't hit you with this one straight away because this task can be daunting if you have some clutter. Grab your recycle bin, trash can, and cleaner and get to work. Clear all the clutter. Remove paper and objects you don't use or need, and file papers in a filing cabinet or filing box that helps you feel organized. Once everything is off the desktop, clean it thoroughly before putting your items back. Make sure to clean and dust your computers, keyboards, microphones, and other electronics with appropriate tools, rags, and cleaners that don't damage them! Read the instructions if you don't know what to use.

5. Arrange useful objects within reach. If the writing space is easy to use and has all your favorite tools within arm's reach, this will

be a place you love to sit. And that is the goal here! What do you use often? What can be kept in a drawer or cabinet? Try different arrangements until you love the way it feels.

6. Decorate with color and manifesting objects. You want your writing to feel inspired, easy, powerful, and prolific. So, does the decor in your room inspire you? Make you feel at ease? Help your flow? You can use paint colors, artwork, special pens, candles, books, quotes, or other sacred objects you love to inspire your writing space. Make this yours!

7. Privacy. When you write in a noisy room, the distractions can get in the way of your flow. Assess the location of your writing space to see if you need to change it up and create more quiet and privacy for your sacred writing time.

8. Speaking of distractions, get in the habit of unplugging before you write. Exit out of all other screens on your computer and make sure the notification noises are off. Put your phone somewhere you can't see the screen lighting up with texts. Turn the ringer off. If you have a landline phone, unplug it. If you have a person in your house who is famous for interrupting just when you get into the flow, make a little sign and post it outside your door: "Please be quiet, sacred writing in progress!"

9. Your writing time. Everyone is more productive during different times of the day, so figure out your best time for writing and creating, and then protect that time on your calendar. I hope you look forward to sitting in your sacred space as a VIP appointment with yourself. I'm an early morning person. When I don't honor that, my writing suffers or feels tight or constricted.

10. Extras. Do you love to write to music? What kind? Do you have a speaker that connects to your phone or computer so you can play your favorite inspirational music? How about that essential oil that helps you feel uplifted or inspired? I love my DoTerra oils! I change them out in my diffuser depending on my mood and goal for the day. Do you drink a special tea? How about brewing a cup before

you sit to write? I love Tea Pigs teas. The "Happy" and "Calm" are two of my faves.

When you have a sacred writing space you love, your energy will be different (more joyful, easier, more relaxed), and that is the same energy you'll be infusing into your brave words. It's also the same energy your readers will feel when they read your beautiful writing. So, what do you want them to feel?

Set up your sacred writing space to give you the advantage of helping *yourself* feel all those same things first! Your writing will never be the same! And your readers won't be able to put your writing down! Changing the world with your brave words starts with nourishing the sacred space for your writing.

Now that you have a sacred, dedicated space for your writing and manifesting, you can practice many powerful writing exercises that will clear and open a space for a high-vibe flow of manifesting energy. Let's start with gratitude and love!

12.

Be Grateful, But Also Know What You Love

Get ready to have your gratitude list practice up-leveled.

Gratitude is the magical starter energy that helps pull people out of their sadness, fear, or anxiety quickly. So, if you're starting from a lower vibe today, gratitude is a great way to go, because gratitude, fear, and other low vibes can't co-exist at the same time. If you're in gratitude, you're already halfway there. And. . .

Ever hear of a love list? When I was prompted to create love lists instead of gratitude lists, my entire practice took a leap into high-vibe land. I felt it immediately. It was like when I tell my authors to "power up" their words in a bio or other passage about themselves. We can either use mediocre words, or we can power them up to words that express a deeper or more intense feeling.

What do you love? I'll get you writing about this in a moment, but first, imagine one thing (person, circumstance, object, environment, it doesn't matter) you love. You might even close your eyes and meditate on it for a few moments.

Bring in the vision of this thing in all its glory and senses. What does this thing you love smell and taste like? What does it look, sound, and feel like? Vision it now. Bring the experience of it into your body and mind.

Experience it without having it in front of you, because the marvelous brain doesn't know the difference!

Look at you, you're raising your vibe already!

Now, imagine some way you love to feel. This is a bit different. It's not the thing you love, it's the way you feel as a result of it. What ways do you love to feel?

"OMG, I love feeling excited about this new book we're launching," I told a friend. "This excitement feels like pure inspiration; it feels all bubbly inside! I have full-body goosebumps!"

The things you love create high-vibe feelings, and that is powerful manifesting energy.

I love my gratitude lists. If you looked at my old journals, you'd see lots of gratitude lists. And while I believe that was a step in the right direction, nobody ever told me to take it a step further and actually feel the feels of those things, or do anything else but write them down.

Now that I know the power of combining my journaling and lists with feelings, both in written and practical form, I have a superpower.

So, let's make a love list. There are two versions, but take my prompts and then do with them what you will after that. I've even created art that hangs in my office based on these lists. The trick is the words and energy that you remind yourself to create!

Let's Write

Remember to do your body and mind awareness practice (even if it's three breaths' worth) before you write. Set your timer for three minutes and write as fast as you can without censoring yourself. If three minutes isn't enough, give yourself as much time as needed and write until you're complete. You'll often notice a natural pause where the writing slows and finishes.

The Prompt

This is a list-making prompt. Write as many things down in your list as you can think of:

1. I love _____.

2. I love feeling _____.

When you're done with your lists, you might consider putting some of them in special places in different areas. I have one of my lists on my phone Notes function to grab whenever I need it. And I have some versions in art and sticky note form in my office, bathroom, and kitchen.

Room to write. . .

13.

Question Everything You Think

In a continued effort to Feng Shui my soul with my writing, I question everything. I often ask myself, "Do you believe that?"

"Why do you believe that?" is another good question. Typically, I can trace back every single thing I believe to a moment in time when I learned it from some person or circumstance. And many times, I realize all my beliefs are based on what I made up in my head through a filter of childhood experiences. They say that is happening up until about five to seven years of age, depending on who you read.

I have trouble remembering much of my childhood. There are some specific memories of places we lived, and friends I had, but where and how I began to believe certain things about myself and life is foggy.

If you want a great listen on this topic, come hear Kyle Cease talk about this: https://youtu.be/2s9T2xs0Ezc

When Kyle talked about the fact that we're all just five-year-olds walking around being triggered from that five-year-old place, life made a ton more sense to me. And I started to wonder if anything I believe is "right." What feels truer now is:

Everything I believe is my truth in the moment, is based on the life I've lived. It doesn't make it true or right for everyone.

Everyone makes judgments based on what they've lived. That's necessary to survive. But when we fall into a trap of thinking our truth is what's right, we get into a struggle with people. I realized my five-year-old reactions (especially of not feeling worthy) weren't serving my warrior goddess empire-building vision and mission. I had to pause, take a breath, and start questioning myself and those around me. Being curious is a superpower.

Whoa, is that true? This is me in my head after hearing a client describe a scenario she had communicating with one of my team members.

Get all the info. Make sure you talk to everyone. Remember, the more communication the better! I reminded myself not to react, but to research first. To breathe before jumping to assumptions or conclusions.

Everyone makes judgments. We're all doing the best we can with what we have in the moment we're in, with the life we've lived up until now. When we know that, we can be a little softer with our judgments.

Questioning everything (especially when I caught myself in the middle of some heavy judgment) was a big move I made toward letting go and detaching from outcomes—two other powerful pieces of my awareness practice. They all go together.

Here are some personal reactions that manifested as thoughts in my head when I was faced with a scenario and caught myself in judgment:

That's (she/he's) crazy!
That's bullshit.
No way is that how it is!
What the fuck?
Wow, I have no idea what they're talking about.
Who does he think he is?
What was he/she thinking?
Holy crap, really?

Pay attention to your own reactions, and you'll have a key to when to substitute curiosity.

Here's a better way to turn this around and ask questions that help you with clarity:

Wow, that's interesting. I wonder why they said what they said?
That's not what I expected. Let me get more information.

I'm not sure I totally understand. I'll ask for a conversation.
What can I learn from this?
What's the lesson in this scenario?
What do I need to know to feel better about this?

Being curious is a superpower. Questioning everything you think allows you to stay open to possibilities, new solutions, and brand-new ways of thinking about a topic. It's the way we innovate. It's the way the world evolves and advances.

Do you have your curiosity hat on today?

Let's Write

Remember to do your body and mind awareness practice (even if it's three breaths' worth) before you write. Set your timer for three minutes and write as fast as you can without censoring yourself. If three minutes isn't enough, give yourself as much time as needed and write until you're complete. You'll often notice a natural pause where the writing slows and finishes.

The Prompt

1. What do you know you're right about? Why or how do you know you're right?

2. Take a moment to read what you wrote. If there were another way to think about it, what would that be? Just play with possibilities here.

I love journaling on topics I know I'm right about to see if that bigger Source inside has a solution I haven't thought about yet. Ask yourself: What else is possible? And let that thought lead you through your day.

Next, we'll discover a powerful way to deal with the inner critic messages that limit our dream life.

Room to write. . .

_____

_____

_____

_____

_____

_____

_____

_____

_____

_____

_____

_____

_____

_____

_____

_____

_____

_____

_____

_____

_____

14.

How to Transform Negative Self-Talk

"Give that voice a name."

One moment in a writer's retreat changed my awareness game, and I transformed my relationship with self-sabotaging thoughts and self-talk. This forever helped me discern between a voice I should follow and one I need to take with a grain of salt.

Martha is my inner critic's name. It's what came through when I asked that question in the bathroom mirror that day. Martha was the name of my maternal grandmother.

For me, the idea was more about generational healing and ancestral lineage. It was about the DNA carried down the line and, within it, the secrets to enlightenment. Yeah, it was a big deal!

Take a moment to think about the inner critic voices and messages that come through for you. Can you name your voice?

When you make space by naming the voice, you can observe the message and respond, rather than react to it. Naming the inner critic will help you step back and have an aware conversation with it, rather than getting caught up in emotion. With awareness, you'll know the difference between a self-sabotaging thought and one that's aligned with your soul's calling.

Here are several ways to discern your inner critic voice so you can begin to transform it:

- The inner critic voice never feels good.

- The inner critic voice is always worried, fearful, anxiety-filled, or doubting.

- Even if it has your best interests at heart, the inner critic is always low-vibe.

- Inner critic messages are usually negative and paralyzing.

- The inner critic sounds like someone who knows better and is trying to warn you.

- Messages from the inner critic feel like impostor syndrome-ish.

- Messages from your inner critic feel constricting in your body.

Inner critic messages are an opportunity to up-level your awareness and choose a different thought, belief, or habit. You can befriend this inner critic (which is often ego) and help it feel safe. It's not about ignoring it or banishing it. It's about helping it feel heard.

I found multiple versions of the voice inside me. One was very negative and always reminded me of the bad things in any situation. The other was a presence that didn't have a voice—a little girl hiding from the world, afraid of speaking up at all. And one of the voices sounded like my ex: explaining the right way to do everything and how I did it wrong.

Awareness changes everything.

The voice of your soul, intuition, higher power, or Source—those messages are divinely inspired, full of excitement and inspiration, and feel good. They feel channeled, in the flow, and come easily and generously. They surprise you. They feel different.

Know the difference. Because when you're in the process of writing your dream life, you'll even notice them on the page. When you discern between them, you will have another writing superpower and can choose which to believe, which to follow, and which to align with moving forward.

The prompt in this chapter contains the first and second steps of awareness for moving the inner critic out and preventing it from taking up precious real estate in your body-mind.

Let's Write

Remember to do your body and mind awareness practice (even if it's three breaths' worth) before you write. Set your timer for three minutes and write as fast as you can without censoring yourself. If three minutes isn't enough, give yourself as much time as needed and write until you're complete. You'll often notice a natural pause where the writing slows and finishes.

The Prompt

1. What are some of the inner critic messages that limit you? Write down all the versions you can think of.

2. If this voice had a name, what would it be?

3. Write your inner critic a letter. Begin with "Dear [name], I understand you're trying to help me, but I got this _____."

Next, get ready to do one of the most powerful awareness exercises there is: getting a clear answer to any question you have.

Room to write. . .

15.

How to Never Doubt Again

[Note: The following is an excerpt from my chapter in *Sacred Spaces* by lead author Colleen Avis. This is a longer chapter because it's important, and I want you to get the full picture.]

I found the secret to being clear about every single decision in my life, and it has nothing to do with thinking. Well, maybe a little thinking about how you're feeling.

Body awareness is the secret. Feeling everything and creating a practice of discernment of those feelings provides a magical cheat sheet for knowing when to say yes, when to say no, how to set boundaries, and how to **never be confused again.**

"I'm not sure this is right for me; I'll think about it and get back to you."

"Okay, let's talk in a couple of days. Let me know if you have any questions."

I'm calling person A out on their bullshit right now. They *do* know—it's not right. They just want to help person B feel okay in the moment, so they're going to delay the decision for now, even though they know it's a no.

I've been person A so many times, wanting to overthink a decision to see if it's right for me because it's the nice or right thing to do. The thing is, "I'm not sure it's right" has always meant "it's not right." Never has it been right. Never. Out of some twisted form of people-pleasing or obligatory conditioning, I said yes, only to regret that decision later and have to deal with the consequences. Ugh. No more.

It would've been so much easier to move through the pain of, "No, thank you, this isn't for me," right away. I can feel the relief in my gut and heart just thinking about it.

You've most likely been in this scenario, either as person A or person B. Probably both at one point or another. If you're person A, you already know the answer; you're just scared to deliver it, afraid you'll offend, upset, or disappoint someone.

And if you're person B, you already know their authentic answer because you can feel the uncertainty, doubt, or foggy nature of the way they're behaving. You know it's a no. And that's good because you can move on—if they'd only be brave enough to tell you.

What if there were nobody left to offend, upset, or disappoint—*poof,* they're gone. What would you think, say, or do? What big-ass dream would you curate? The good news: You only have yourself to prove things to. Nobody else matters. Honor yourself first. The rest of the world can come next.

I've said yes to many things out of duty, obligation, or people-pleasing. This was horrible for me, and it wasn't great for the other person either. I probably fooled myself by thinking they couldn't see through my energy. I know they did. So can you. You feel it immediately. It's just that you're so used to second-guessing that feeling, trained to ignore it and manipulate it into something else, that you're blinded. You think you're doing someone a favor when really, you're just making everything more difficult, complicated, and chaotic.

Here are my conditioned thoughts when in the middle of these scenarios:

I owe them this.

*This is what I **should** do.*

Oh, that S-word!

They'll be so happy if I say yes.

Maybe *they* will, but how about you?

I feel so bad; I'll just say yes.

Guilt is a tricky thing.

They are my (mother, father, sister, friend, spouse, family), so I have to.

Wanna know what saying yes when I meant no got me? Chest pains, anxiety, and exhaustion. It got me sick, y'all.

Who do we think we're helping when we say yes, even though we mean no? How's that going down in the end after we've spent every last morsel of time, energy, dollars, or effort, and there's none left for us?

The oxygen mask is nowhere to be found. You crashed already.

Stop your people-pleasing, please.

Be deliciously selfish today. What serves you? What joy, love, or gratitude can you bring into your life right now? Make sure you're pleasing yourself. Make sure you're filling your tank with high-vibe energy, and say yes to things that create that fuel. Anything else is draining or toxic.

One note about the stuff in life we don't seem to get to choose: With awareness, you still get a choice.

So even if you'd typically say no but can't, there's a way to move through it.

During my daughter's trial against her abuser, I had to survive through what I had no choice about. I was a witness for the prosecution. And I knew the questions weren't going to put me in the best light. I prepared to be shamed. What I was forced to say yes to was from an intense (heart-felt) obligation to my daughter and her mental and physical health. There was no choice.

Or was there?

"Ms. Di Franco, can you please try to answer the question?"

The judge repeated this about three times. The defense attorney had asked me something my mind-body went completely blank about.

I sat for a very uncomfortable amount of time, silent. My chest tightened. The entire room, including the judge, stared and waited for me to speak. I felt my throat tighten, my gut clench, and my back arch a bit on the hard wooden chair. I took a sip of water.

You can slow down. You don't need to make everyone happy right now. Slow down. Breathe.

My mind raced uncontrollably, looking for some kind of answer. But there was none. He asked me a question I couldn't answer.

I took a very long, deep breath. I think I sighed, but I don't remember any noise.

I kept breathing and reached into my right pocket to run my thumb and fingers over the rose quartz heart I kept there, *just in case.*

I let them all squirm for a few more breaths.

You're not going to die. Take another breath.

I did. I got back into my body.

"I'm sorry, I don't know how to answer this question. Can you ask it in a different way?"

Thank you to our attorney for coaching that last response.

"No further questions, your honor."

The defense attorney finished, and now it was time to answer the questions I'd waited four years to answer from our side. Our gal stepped up to the desk microphone, and my back and gut clench softened. She looked me in the eye *(I have your back)* and took another big pause. I wanted to cry but choked it back.

She did have my back.

"Laura, can you remember. . ."

By the way, y'all. We won the case.

There will be times when this thing I'm asking you to do—you know, feel things— seems impossible. That's reality. There will be times you step up for others and are forced to take actions you wouldn't otherwise volunteer for. That's life. If you're a parent (or human) who cares, you'll face many of these moments.

You survive by prioritizing all your *other* moments. Find the brave spaces in between the rest of the difficult ones, and focus there.

When I sat in the tiny holding room waiting to be called to the witness stand, a room (place and circumstance) I didn't choose or ask for, I felt literal pain. The combination of mental fuckery (anxiety, fear, doubt, repetitive worst-case scenarios) tightened my chest, gut, and jaw. But I couldn't walk out. I couldn't leave the room. I wouldn't let my daughter down.

I practiced prioritizing the moment I was in with a few tools to bring higher vibes into my heart. I breathed *a lot*. I did a number countdown, 50 to one. I put some sound-healing music on my headphones. I pet Josiah (the therapy dog) a lot. *You're not on the witness stand yet,* I reminded myself. With that awareness, I chose moments to serve me in between the ones I didn't sign up for. I found my brave spaces and shifted into my body.

Sometimes, that's all you have.

However, in normal life circumstances, you usually have *many* more opportunities to unapologetically choose and prioritize yourself. It's not selfish. It *serves* others to serve yourself. It generously serves others to live from an overflow of time, money, energy, positivity, and resources.

Get into your body and make your decisions from there. Let's do this together.

Where are your brave spaces?

* * *

The one simple exercise I'll guide you through changed my life. It helped me get in touch with the most powerful force for decision-making there is: the body.

When we leave our body and land in the overthinking mind, we leave all our power behind and end up paralyzed in some dark, ruminating space that'll never ever serve our hearts and souls.

Grounded and centered in powerful body awareness is where every decision can be made from a crystal-clear place, one that's aligned with your heart and soul and best serves you and everyone else.

It serves them *because* it serves you.

Let's Write

Note: If getting into your body is difficult or impossible because of past trauma, then find expert guidance to help hold a sacred, safe space for your journey. This is so important. Seek out a trauma-informed expert therapist or coach and get support so you can connect to your power again.

Be Bodyful—the Journaling Exercise for Making Every Decision Easy

What you'll need: A piece of paper (normal spiral notebook size), a pen, and some time without distractions. Put your phone on "Do Not Disturb."

Draw a line down the middle of your piece of paper, making two columns. Label the top on the left "YES!" Label the top on the right "NO!"

Start on the right with the "NO" column.

Think about when something feels bad, uncertain, not aligned, or not for you. Think about when it's a "no." Think about people, places, or circumstances that feel like they go against what you stand for or make you feel sad, fearful, cloudy, or bad.

What do those things feel like in your body? Begin to describe them by making a list of those descriptive words in the "NO" column on the right side of your page.

Some of mine are:

Tight
Cold
Shriveled
Closed

Give yourself a couple of minutes to write down as many descriptive words as you can think of. If you write words like "bad" or "confused," think about where "bad" or "confused" is located in your body and describe how that feels instead. The "NO" has a feeling. See if you can connect with the sensation of what you feel in your body with a "NO."

Now, go over to the "YES" column on the left.

Think about what something fully aligned with your heart and soul feels like in your body. Think about the things and circumstances in your life that you love. Think of what you were born for: things, people, places, or circumstances aligned with your purpose that turn you on and that help you feel happy, uplifted, and joyful.

What does that feel like in your body?

Begin to describe them by making a list of those descriptive words in the "YES" column on the left side of your page.

Some of mine are:

Flexible
Light
Warm
Spacious

Give yourself a couple of minutes to write down as many descriptive words as you can think of. If you write words like "happy" or "energized," think about where "happy" or "energized" is showing up in your body and describe how that feels instead. The "YES" has a feeling, a posture, and body language. See if you can connect with what happens in your body with a "YES."

At the end of this exercise, you'll have a pretty badass cheat sheet to refer to any time you're wondering if something you're considering is a "yes" or a "no."

***

"Mary, I'm confused about this. I don't know what to do."

I said this to my very talented and wise healer friend during a session one day.

"It's easier to be confused," she said. "It's harder to make a decision and take action about what you already know you need to do."

I had one of the biggest *aha* moments of my life that day.

I realized that when you're trying to make a decision, and it feels confusing, foggy, unclear, or uncertain, guess what? It's a no.

Because *confusing, foggy, unclear,* and *uncertain* all have a feeling in the body, and they certainly aren't a "YES!"

Now, whenever I find myself wanting to say to someone, "I'm not sure this is right for me; I'll think about it and get back to you," I immediately catch myself in that very clear moment. It's not a yes, so it's a no, or maybe it's a "Not right now."

Being clear about that helps me take action that's aligned, authentic, and straightforward and serves me and everyone I'm involved with. Clear is kind.

This is a ninja move of awareness and discernment. It's why I prefer being bodyful rather than mindful. My body is the place to listen for the answers.

The next way I want you to write to Feng Shui your soul is by busting through purpose-driven fear on the way to writing your dream life!

Room to write. . .

_____

_____

_____

_____

_____

_____

_____

_____

_____

_____

_____

_____

_____

_____

_____

_____

_____

_____

_____

_____

_____

16.

Fear-Busting Badassery

What are some of the fears that keep you from going for the life you dream of? Get on your awareness hat, and think back to some of the exercises you've already done in this book. There are survival-type fears, and then there are the kind we have when we're going for something big (or some kind of change), and we're excited-scared. These fears are attached to moments, thoughts, or goals we have for our life that are fully aligned with our soul. They're what our soul keeps pulling us to (even if it feels like that survival kind of fear in our gut).

Awareness, awareness, awareness.

Breathe and drop down into your body. Fear is a feeling that you're making mean something. When you start to make it mean something, fear steals your show. Strip away the thoughts and meaning, and you're left with a sensation in your body.

Back in March of 2020, for about a week after the pandemic shut down my physical therapy practice, I was panicked! The income from that practice was how I took care of myself and my kids. I was divorced and had to provide for myself, pay the mortgage, and support my two kids headed to college. I wanted to pivot to my Brave Healer Productions business and told people, "I'm transitioning to it," for about five years—only I was too afraid to do it. That purpose-driven fear was paralyzing. When the pandemic forced the transition, I felt relieved. I had no choice but to make it happen. And I did (of course!). I wish I'd done it sooner.

The Universe brought many signs before that year. The ideas were always inspired, flowed easily (and furiously), and circled back over and over. These are some of the ways I feel the purpose-driven kind of fear now. This kind of fear shows up in different ways, but most always forces me into a feeling of excitement about what's possible.

To bust through fear and align with your dreams, you need to focus on a couple of things. You need to understand your dreams and desires, and whether they're authentic (aligned with your soul's purpose). If your dreams are based on what the rest of the world told you you should want to be happy, you have some work to do. And, secondly, you have to get good at feeling, awareness, and pausing before you react.

Busting through purpose-driven fear requires a full knowledge of your values, desires, and vision for your life, and it requires ninja-level mind-body awareness.

You can use all your purpose-driven fear as fuel and write your dream life into reality.

I wrote an entire book on this subject. I hope you'll go pick up a copy of *How to Have Fun With Your Fear* if you need more than this short chapter. I loved the challenge of getting the basics into this shorter chapter, though. Because dealing with your fears (the purpose-driven kind) can be easier than you think.

Let's Write

Remember to do your body and mind awareness practice (even if it's three breaths' worth) before you write. Set your timer for three minutes and write as fast as you can without censoring yourself. If three minutes isn't enough, give yourself as much time as needed and write until you're complete. You'll often notice a natural pause where the writing slows and finishes.

The Prompt

Spend 3 minutes on each:

1. What I truly desire in my life right now is _____. Don't hold back. This should have nothing to do with what anyone else has taught you you should want. This should be a purely selfish list that brings you full joy.

2. The values important to me and how I live my life are _____.

3. _____ scares me because _____.

4. If I move through my fears and do _____, I will feel _____.

There are many different versions of purpose-driven fears. Basically, if the fear is coming from a place inside that feels purposeful and excitement is the overpowering emotion, then it's purpose-driven fear—the kind you should pay attention to and begin to make friends with so you can overcome it. Doubt, worry, and anxiety are forms of these kinds of fears. Let's tackle those next.

Room to write. . .

_____

_____

_____

_____

_____

_____

_____

_____

_____

_____

_____

_____

_____

_____

_____

_____

_____

_____

_____

_____

17.

Clearing Doubt, Worry, and Anxiety

Doubt, worry, and anxiety are often purpose-driven fears or ruminating thoughts you're stuck in. Most of the time, they result in our mind moving to past or future moments, rather than being fully in the present. When it comes to writing your dream life, it's awesome to have a handle on doubt, worry, and anxiety, and especially to know how to put laser focus on the power of the present moment to alleviate those feelings.

"Your anxiety can be grief."

Remember this line? That idea gave me an *aha,* which changed the way I moved forward with my feelings of anxiety. I found relief in connecting the two. It gave me permission to observe the anxiety differently—not try to push it away or get rid of it, but to be gentler with it.

Trying to get rid of a feeling is often what makes it worse.

"Worrying is like praying for something you don't want to happen." I used this in Chapter 6 to help you be more aware of the self-sabotaging nature of worry.

Ruminating worry thoughts aren't helpful. Worse, they focus on negative thoughts and energy that attract more like it. When I start to worry about something, I have a toolkit I reach into to shift the energy because: **Everything is attraction.**

In the game of writing your dream life, knowing everything is attraction is a weighty responsibility. Some days, I'd rather not know and just be oblivious to this little fact. It's hard to know this. Knowing sometimes creates stress because many days, it's challenging to shift out of worry thoughts.

In Dr. Wayne Dyer's book *Excuses Begone,* there's a brilliant chapter that coaches us in this way: If you're not 100% sure a situation is going to end up in a positive outcome, but you're also not 100% sure it will end up negative, then while you're waiting, imagine the positive outcome.

This is kinda Law of Attraction 101. Adopt the positive mindset and vibe in that higher frequency until the outcome occurs. Because in the waiting, it certainly can't hurt you to think positively. In contrast, a negative focus can hurt you. Worrying obsessively about everything creates stress, and stress has a negative physiological effect on the body.

How often do you catch yourself worrying? You now have an idea of the opportunity you have. Turning that worry time into meditation, or even better, into affirmation of your desires, dreams, and goals, will be a game-changer.

When writing doesn't help, I clean. The Feng Shui of cleaning is a direct energy shifter. It's physical movement (which helps on its own), and it's energetic clearing of your environment, which also shifts the energy in a positive way.

Let's do a little clearing with our writing first.

Let's Write

Remember to do your body and mind awareness practice (even if it's three breaths' worth) before you write. Set your timer for three minutes and write as fast as you can without censoring yourself. If three minutes isn't enough, give yourself as much time as needed and write until you're complete. You'll often notice a natural pause where the writing slows and finishes.

The Prompt

1. Write down your worries. All of them. Move them out of your head and onto the paper.

2. Start a new page. Write the words, "I'm so happy and grateful now that _____." Write out the situation as though you're living it inside of the solution. Write the positive outcome and feel it as you're living it in the moment of powerfully writing it.

The "I'm so happy and grateful now that" writing prompt is a game-changer for shifting a worry to a solution. It's a way to live positively in the moment. Write your dream life by shifting each worry into a powerful mantra of ease, gratitude, joy, power, or love.

Let's get to a few more things to Feng Shui to continue to clear out what's in the way of our dream life.

Room to write. . .

18.

No More Guilt, Obligation, Shoulds, or Supposed-tos

"Just because they're family doesn't mean you have an obligation to them. If they're toxic, you have to take care of yourself," said Robin, looking at me with her calm, blue eyes.

"Yeah, but. . ." I interrupted.

What's the "yeah but" for you?

In the above conversation, I was talking to one of my healers about the obligation I felt to be nice and attempt to engage in a relationship with my dad, even though I never felt good in his presence.

It took years to want to call him. I wanted to want to. But I wasn't willing to abandon my own soul. I had to love myself enough first.

I remember a couple of moments on the spiritual journey when I was filled with unconditional love and forgiveness. I realized that work didn't mean I was obligated to communicate or try to have a relationship. I felt good about doing the work energetically and released a lot of the guilt and obligation, whether or not I spoke with him.

Before he died, I spoke to him a few times a year—Father's Day, his birthday, my birthday, sometimes Christmas or Thanksgiving. I worked to make those phone calls happen from a place of genuine desire and love, rather than obligation.

You might be in a similar place of wondering:

"Yeah, but it's my daughter."

"Yeah, but it's my mom."

"Yeah, but it's my _____."

The thing is, we're taught some pretty specific things about what we're supposed to think or do when it comes to family. We're taught we have an obligation to family over everyone else, including ourselves.

I think this is wrong. We have an obligation to ourselves first. If we don't prioritize our own health, wellness, and wealth, any service we try to give to anyone else is lacking. If we burn out or experience illness or disease, the obligation to serve others isn't going to mean much.

I look around at so many people in the middle of people-pleasing disasters. Their health declines, yet they won't prioritize their own health because of the duty and obligation they feel to the other person. It's such a catch-22. When I live my life based on duty, obligation, shoulds, or supposed-tos, I live in a messy mashup of guilt, frustration, resentment, and even anger.

"I don't do anger," my friend Ilene says. "It's such a waste of time!"

I agree with Ilene, and when I heard her say that, I was intrigued and leaned in. *What would a life without guilt and anger look like?*

A lot like peace, I imagine.

Obligatory actions became a GPS system for me in my body. It's what we do when we say yes but mean no because we're afraid someone will be disappointed in us. Being able to discern between this feeling and other awareness is a game-changer. It's one of those feelings I'm Feng Shui'ing more and more.

What would a life without guilt feel like? A life where you were able to generously take care of yourself without feeling like you were short-changing anyone else, where you fulfilled your purpose without feeling obligations?

Let's Write

Remember to do your body and mind awareness practice (even if it's three breaths' worth) before you write. Set your timer for three minutes and write as fast as you can without censoring yourself. If three minutes isn't enough, give yourself as much time as needed and write until you're complete. You'll often notice a natural pause where the writing slows and finishes.

The Prompt

If there was nobody left to offend, upset, or disappoint, I would _____.

And, what are you waiting for?

Next, we'll tackle one of the most paralyzing problems out there when it comes to self-sabotage: impostor syndrome. Think you're not good enough? Let's stop that, shall we?

Room to write. . .

19.

Purpose-Driven Fear (Impostor Syndrome)

"Your Fear is Boring." This title of a blog by Elizabeth Gilbert gave me pause. It talked me out of impostor syndrome pretty quickly. I vowed: *You will not let your boring fear of not-good-enough take over for one more day.* I turned her statement to, "Your fear of not-good-enough is boring."

My awareness practice up until this point was pretty good—a reliable tool to help me go for joy more often. I learned the difference between a yes and a no and cleared out the rest of the not-joy things from my life, for the most part. My writing practice thrived.

Then I signed up for a mastermind with other-level income earners and realized just how not-through I was with impostor syndrome.

I don't fit in here.
They think I'm stupid.
Nobody is vibing with me.

I started calling myself a visionary alien because I felt the freak factor intensely every time I arrived in the Zoom room with these people. I spent a lot of time trying to understand and accept that alien in me, and love her even though she seemed to scare people.

You scare people, Laura. You're too direct. Why can't you be gentler with people?

When you get thrown back into worrying about what people think, you have to realize you've hit another upper limit—and it's time to up-level your mindset, *again*.

My purpose-driven fears have taken that path, cycling back to make sure I'm rid of them—or at least, that I don't let them trigger me to the point of paralysis.

What a waste of time impostor syndrome is. Think about it: The moment you get derailed—thrown off your track of purpose and good in the world—nobody is helped. The moment you let what others think (or what you think they think) stop you from shining and sharing your brilliance, no lives are changed.

Feng Shui impostor syndrome out of your mind and life. Today. Choose a tool to get to it faster, to hone your awareness to the point that when a whisper of it slides in to taunt you, you notice—and are already on track to focus on something much more helpful.

If you want more guidance, you'll find *How to Have Fun With Your Fear* on Amazon. I wrote that book because of the feelings of impostor syndrome and self-sabotage constantly paralyzing me from truly going for my big dreams. This fear of not being good enough, of not having enough, of constantly being in a "what if this happens" mindset started to annoy me.

Lately, I've noticed something new about impostor syndrome. It shows up when I perceive I'm in a room of people who are more successful than me, and in a thought that sounds like: *I don't have anything to offer these people*. I'm quickly learning that this is a huge opportunity to suspend judgment, stop making assumptions, and just be myself. "Thanks Martha, but I got this!"

Having a daily ritual of cleaning and clearing purpose-driven fear from your mind and energy is essential to writing your dream life. I use my notebooks to move the thoughts and energy out. I love to combine journaling with things like sage burning, candle burning, and essential oil diffusing. Create your own Feng Shui rituals to curate your spaces, both inner and outer.

Go write!

Let's Write

Remember to do your body and mind awareness practice (even if it's three breaths' worth) before you write. Set your timer for three minutes and write as fast as you can without censoring yourself. If three minutes isn't enough, give yourself as much time as needed and write until you're complete. You'll often notice a natural pause where the writing slows and finishes.

The Prompt

1. Write a letter to your younger self. What words of love or advice do you have for her (at any stage) to help her heal from impostor syndrome, or any other type of purpose-driven fear?

2. If I wasn't afraid, I would _____.

So far, we've focused on awareness and using writing to Feng Shui our inner world—the foundations of writing your dream life into reality. With awareness, you have a choice. The more awareness and discernment you have on every subject, the better. Awareness, including the superpowers of listening to your inner voice and intuition, and fine-tuning your claircognizance (clear knowing), will help you live an extraordinary life.

In Part 3 (Write to Align) and Part 4 (Write to Manifest), we take the next steps in using our writing and awareness practices to achieve clarity and alignment. It's in alignment with Source energy, where the magic of receiving and manifestation happens. When our default is that alignment, then writing and living in manifestation mode also become the norm.

Writing your dream life into reality is about the practice and discipline of awareness, and it's time to become unapologetic about how you live, breathe, and be in the world. This path is a love warrior's path. It's the journey of my Brave Healers. It's how we decide to turn our pain into purpose, drop all victim mentality, break all the old molds, and experience what's possible for our lives and the world.

Yes, it's big-potatoes stuff!

Feng Shui practices added into the next two sections will be more about curating your spaces for maximum alignment and magnetism.

Room to write. . .

_____

_____

_____

_____

_____

_____

_____

_____

_____

_____

_____

_____

_____

_____

_____

_____

_____

_____

_____

_____

_____

_____

Part 3

Write to Align

When I'm aligned with Source, I am my highest Self and can receive
anything I desire. It's all a matter of focus.

What are you focused on?

20.

Your Deepest Desires

We've done a lot of awareness work so far. Are you feeling the shift, the awakening, and the power? I'm excited because I know what that enhanced awareness does and the foundation it sets for manifestation! Good job so far! It's not easy work!

The next foundation for manifestation is knowing what you want. Seems silly, but it's crucial, and that changes over your lifetime.

I've never taken the time to ask myself what I really want. Everything I think I want comes from what I've been taught I should want to make me happy.

Over the years, what I wanted changed. That's normal. The biggest awareness of my life came in this moment of realization.

Waking up in a moment like that can be scary. We're talking decades going by before this *aha*. I was in my 30s. House, job, retirement fund, marriage, kids, cars. . .*Really?*

Go ahead, ask me: "Laura, what do you really want?"

Peace. I want the feeling of peace coursing through my body, and I want it daily.

Written for you, *Write Your Dream Life*-style:

I love the feeling of peace, how it flows in and through my body, softening everything, helping my whole body-mind relax into the joy of being alive.

At this point in the book, I'm going to write in a way that you'll notice the shift. What you must understand is that every word counts, written or spoken. Slow your thinking (and writing) train down and be intentional. Every word is a magic spell. Every effort manifests your life. It's time to align with joy (and a few other good-feeling things).

I love the feeling of love.
I love feeling joy.
I love the smile on my face when I'm excited to be alive.
I love feeling grateful.
I love the feeling of gratitude as I take a full, deep breath.
I love feeling peace about my life.
I love knowing the Universe has my back every step of the way and that no matter what, everything is happening for me.
Everything is working out.

If you aren't in the habit of listening to Esther Hicks' channel on YouTube, I highly suggest you put those on your daily listen list. Esther's rampages got me through a dark night of the soul, and even better, are consistent tools for bringing me out of a moment of doubt and pivoting me to receiving mode, which is where I desire to be.

Knowing what you want is part of the trick. And it's the catch-22. When I know what I want, I simultaneously know what I don't have yet. So, aligning with deepest desires is something I want you to practice differently.

I have a money goal for my business that will allow me to write large checks to people and organizations I love. Being aware of that desire also creates an awareness of not being there yet. It's the next step in the process that's the most important: Let go of the ask and bask in the feeling of alignment with Source in any other way possible.

Repeat after me:

"I love having enough money, energy, time, and resources to generously take care of myself and everyone I love and serve."

If it's not true enough for you and creates a feeling of, "But I'm not there yet," then you can get to a place of good-feeling thought that is true for you. That's the first step.

I love the feeling of excitement when I help someone else publish their book! I love feeling this purpose, and I'm so grateful to live that way every day!

That's a very true one for me, no matter how much money is in the bank.

Our writing prompts from here on out will point to the thoughts, energy, and focus that magnetize joy, gratitude, love, and abundance. It's what I want for your practice. Take it to a level where the words you write, speak, and share co-create everything you desire in the moment you share them.

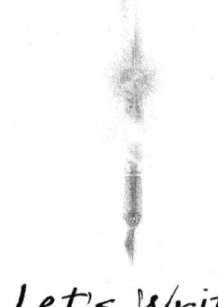

Let's Write

Remember to do your body and mind awareness practice (even if it's three breaths' worth) before you write. Set your timer for three minutes and write as fast as you can without censoring yourself. If three minutes isn't enough, give yourself as much time as needed and write until you're complete. You'll often notice a natural pause where the writing slows and finishes.

Writing "As If"

My favorite way to write my dream life into reality is to write it as if it's happening now, with all the feels. I write and imagine. I write and feel. I write and bask in it, now. Because the brain doesn't know the difference, I know I'm creating a moment of reality every time I practice. This is the energy that manifests.

Writing "as if" starts with any version of, "I'm so happy and grateful now that. . ."

The Prompt

I'm so happy and grateful now that _____.

Use as many details as possible to help get you into the feel of your scene.

Next, we'll use curiosity and big questions to align with what's true for us.

Room to write. . .

_____
_____
_____
_____
_____
_____
_____
_____
_____
_____
_____
_____
_____
_____
_____
_____
_____
_____
_____

Feng Shui

Choose your favorite color(s) and curate your spaces with it. At this point, you may want to reference the Bagua map to relate certain colors to certain areas of your home and play with what lights you up.

My favorite colors are:

_____

_____

_____

_____

_____

Find something in the color you love to add to a space that needs it. How does that color make you feel? Be careful about adding colors that are too stimulating to your bedroom! That room is reserved for calm, peaceful sleep.

I'm going to revisit questions (and questioning everything) in the next chapter. It was an up-leveling of writing my dream life into existence that had great impact.

21.

Questioning Everything

The morning I started feeling chest pain was a wake-up call. I palmed the center of my chest and thought: *OMG, I'm going to have a heart attack and leave my kids motherless.*

I procrastinated about a decision to ask for a divorce despite my body screaming at me. In that moment, my body told me the truth loudly enough to make me pay attention and start asking more important questions.

Curiosity is an awareness superpower, as I already mentioned. But do you know just how powerful it is? It's a magical state of mind that heals relationships and changes lives. In the *aha* moment I mentioned—when I realized I was living a life everyone else taught me to live—I started questioning everything.

When you begin to question every single thing you've ever been taught, something strange, scary, and wonderful happens: You realize nothing is "true." You realize it's all your own truth. You realize the billions of truths out there in the world. And you realize nothing is really as it seems. "It's all an illusion" starts to make sense. And the way you live can change drastically.

This chapter is in the "Alignment" section because I found that the need for this kind of awareness never goes away. We live in a world with lots of people walking around with lots of truths. Authority figures and even friends constantly tell us things we take as truth. Our most trusted friends and colleagues share heartfelt information with us that we believe will help. We lean into it. We lean away from our own inner wisdom and take theirs.

It can be easier to accept what you're told or taught, take it for granted, and live based on that information.

Alignment means feeling for and trusting your own truth.

What personal truths are you ignoring (maybe for a good reason, but still ignoring)? Go back to practice the Yes/No exercise to up-level your body awareness skills.

Let's take this idea and go for more alignment with what's good for our souls. I challenge you to get so good at knowing your truth (from a body awareness perspective) that you can navigate the world, difficult conversations, business deals, friendships, or family dysfunction with confidence and clarity.

Let's Write

Remember to do your body and mind awareness practice (even if it's three breaths' worth) before you write. Set your timer for three minutes and write as fast as you can without censoring yourself. If three minutes isn't enough, give yourself as much time as needed and write until you're complete. You'll often notice a natural pause where the writing slows and finishes.

The Prompt

1. The way I clearly know something is right for me (my truth) is _____.

2. I'm very grateful to have such a powerful GPS system for my soul. When something is right for me, I know it because _____.

Developing trust in these answers and practicing will be a path to powerful manifestation. Next, let's learn how to shift a triggering moment into a manifestation opportunity.

Room to write. . .

_____

_____

_____

_____

_____

_____

_____

_____

_____

_____

_____

_____

_____

_____

_____

_____

_____

_____

_____

_____

Feng Shui

Get curious about your living spaces. Do a home inventory by taking a notepad into each room and making some notes about how certain aspects of each room feel to you. Be curious about what you notice. What feelings do you want to feel? Write those down.

Now you can begin creating new spaces by decluttering, cleaning, clearing, and curating where they're most needed. If a space you're living in doesn't feel awesome, there's an opportunity to raise the vibe! Start with one small room, or even one part of one room, and go from there.

I always focus on rooms I spend the most time in during the day or night: my kitchen, office, and bedroom.

When things don't feel right, or are downright painful, how do we move into alignment? Let's talk about that next.

22.

Pain (Triggers) to Purpose (Alignment)

Recently, I looked at the decades of dusty journals in my plastic bin under the bed and thought: *I've been writing down everything I don't want for years!*

There's nothing wrong with using journals to heal. Narrative therapy is extremely powerful. But (and this is a *but,* not an *and*), what you focus on grows. The power you give something by putting your energy, attention, and intention on it is grand. Be careful what you focus on.

Would I change anything, looking back? No, because I also believe everything before now got me here, and so far, I like it here.

However, if I'd been taught how to wield my magic wand (pen) earlier, I may have used those journals differently, turning my pain into purpose.

Through reading our books and helping all our Brave Healer authors tell their stories, I've gained so much perspective that there's really no moment I experience anymore that doesn't quickly shift into gratitude. Holy cannoli, am I a lucky gal to have read thousands of stories that give me absolutely no excuse to wallow in my pain.

The stories in our books will do that for you. When you need some perspective (I vaguely remember a mentor saying to me one day, "Nobody died."), read something that gives it to you, or talk to someone who has it.

Being triggered is no fun at all. We get pulled into the pit of fear, worry, anxiety, sadness, depression, or anger very quickly, and it's hard to get out when the bottom of the pit feels like quicksand. Awareness is the key here—the entire Part 1 of this book.

Wake up in your trigger and breathe. Clear your mind. Ground and center into the current moment with your breath. Realize where you are, and notice if your thoughts are in the past (regret) or in the future (worry). Neither of those places is where the shift happens. The shift happens in this moment, with a clear mind and fierce attention to the space within you and around you. What do you hear, see, smell?

Might be a great moment to pop on your earphones and play a little sound healing music. Or hum. Yes, hum.

"You can't be both afraid and grateful at the same time."

I interviewed one of the co-authors of our book, *Expressive Arts,* the other day, and when she said this, something clicked for me. I'd heard it before, but she was also talking about the powerful modality of humming, or toning. The vibration we're creating in us with humming creates an inability to experience the lower vibrations of other emotions.

I think I'm going to take up humming more often!

"Does what you're thinking or doing right now align with the big vision for your life?"

This is such a great, in-the-moment gut-check question if something you're saying, thinking, or doing doesn't feel good.

I admit, I ask this a lot when the sixth Oreo enters my mouth at night and the thought, *Don't eat anything after 7:00 p.m.,* slides in to taunt me.

I have a goal of peak performance and fitness. Oreos after seven aren't aligned with that picture. The real question? Can I stay accountable to my own dreams and goals and align with them every day? Or am I going to let old, bad, unhealthy, and unhelpful habits sabotage all that?

Hey, it's tough, I know, and the only real control we have in life is our response to what is.

Has anyone read Byron Katie and her book *Loving What Is?*

I like being in control of my responses, especially when I feel triggered. I feel like a badass mindset ninja when I'm triggered, feel that gut twist, and can respond by moving back to calm and peace with a few breaths. That woman who learned how to do that is someone I admire—my warrior woman.

Pain-to-purpose in the moment is a ninja move. How fast can we get there? Well, with practice, I'd say seconds. A breath. The times the gut twist lasted a week? Oh my, how sad that was. I let the opinion or reaction from another human affect me so much that I was pulled out of my very powerful life's purpose and was paralyzed. No lives changed there.

I don't let that happen for very long anymore.

How can you tighten your response to a trigger?

Let's Write

Remember to do your body and mind awareness practice (even if it's three breaths' worth) before you write. Set your timer for three minutes and write as fast as you can without censoring yourself. If three minutes isn't enough, give yourself as much time as needed and write until you're complete. You'll often notice a natural pause where the writing slows and finishes.

The Prompt

List the thoughts, words, behaviors, actions, and responses that are fully aligned with your values, mission, vision, and purpose. Have fun making this list!

Room to write. . .

Feng Shui

When I first started my Feng Shui practice, I was introduced to simple tools, practices, and even natural cleaning solutions that created small shifts in my energy and mood.

"Try a little peppermint essential oil in warm, soapy water for your front door," said Dana.

OMG, y'all, I was addicted from that first experiment. My front door now gets the royal treatment, including a couple of drops of that peppermint oil. Think about it: The front door is the entryway to your entire home. It's where people and things enter. It's a portal.

Time to grab your bucket of warm, soapy water and your favorite invigorating or activating essential oil and get that front door to sparkle!

In the next few chapters, we'll go deeper into everything you want to align with in your life.

Let's talk about aligning with purpose.

23.

Purpose Exercise

"You give meaning to your purpose."

Do you remember where you first saw or heard this? I do. One of my physical therapy mentors, Tom Baker, said it during a continuing education course.

I went on to have so many conversations with my brave healer friends about this.

"I get that purpose isn't something we're assigned. It's the meaning we give it. Really, when it comes down to it, joy is our purpose. And what brings joy are the breadcrumbs to follow," I said to Barb on Zoom one day.

What do you think about this, dear reader? Have you been searching for purpose in something you do, or a cause to belong to? Have you been searching in all the wrong places?

Another friend, Carole, said, "There's your more human purpose, and then there's your soul's purpose. Knowing the difference is important."

I had to chew on that for a while. It was another game-changing way to think about things I'd learned all my life.

One particular moment will always be one of my biggest turning points in terms of aligning with purpose.

In 2016, a stranger reached out on Facebook Messenger. You might know the Shirley story if you've been in my world long enough. When I met Shirley and realized my purpose had a face and a name, everything changed. At the time, she was a total stranger reaching out on Messenger to ask for more self-care blogs to read. I learned she was a mother of five, and struggling with depression. Through a few more short exchanges, a dedicated blog to her, and the start of a friendship, I realized my writing could have much greater impact than I realized. It could save lives. Shirley eventually confided in me that she'd been writing the suicide note she would share with her husband and five children.

If this is the only thing I ever do with my writing, it is enough.

Here's a poem I wrote about that.

Purpose Has a Face
by Laura Di Franco

You'll find your purpose
when you look in the eyes
of your brother or sister
mother or father
spouse or lover
friend, co-worker or foe
and instead of feeling
distrust or rage
unworthiness, embarrassment, or shame
you recognize yourself
and feel love.

Purpose has a face
and a name.

Find your purpose!
Live in your purpose!
You were born with a purpose!
If I hear this one more time
from one more life coach
as the secret to my happiness

I might just land an axe kick
to the side of their face.

Wondering what I mean?
Surely a purpose-driven life is what's meant to be?
How will we survive without a purpose?
Something to drive us.
Some reason to be.
Some topic of catastrophe
to attach to?
Some cause to lend our hand to?

Y'all. . .purpose has a face.
True purpose
unless it has to do with a living, breathing,
taco-eating human just like us
will never feel complete.

Purpose has a face
and a name.

I'm tired of searching the planet
for my reason for being
in all the wrong places.
Tired of the sprint to success
and achievement
as a means to changing the world.

Purpose has a name.
The man or woman
boy or girl
straight or gay
black or white
rich or poor
married or divorced
human
that gives you reason to know
that your breath

changed their ability to
know their worth.

She is your purpose.
He is your purpose.
They are your purpose.

Change one life
and you change the world.
It's enough.

As you're listening to these words
close your eyes
take a breath. . .

Who has made a difference for you?
Who has made you want to be more of yourself?
Who's loved you no matter what?
Who's told you - "You changed my life!"
Who helped you wake up this morning
with fire in your soul,
ready to be your full-on, badass, unapologetic self?
Let that face come into your mind.

Open your eyes.
Now say a name.

We just changed our purpose game
You claimed the name
who made you know
you were born
so you're worthy,
you matter.
Your presence is the very reason
someone wanted to wake up
another day.

Purpose has a face.
and a name.

I look around
into eyes and smiles
snaps and claps
and sometimes a tear
and I really get it now.

Every single moment you spend
honored by the company of someone who cares
is a moment of true purpose.

Have you been searching too?
You can stop now.
It's not what you do. . .it's a who you're looking for.
Purpose is right in front of you.

If you'd like to listen to a spoken-word version of that poem, please do so here: https://youtu.be/Fo09sioAz9g

For me, over the years, purpose has felt like a combination of pursuing joy and finding fulfillment as I serve the people around me. Joy is the fuel, though. If I'm not joyful in my work, I'm not serving in a sustainable way. If joy isn't what I put in my gas tank, and I'm filling it with supposed-tos and shoulds, I'm going to blow up my engine quickly.

So, with joy as my guide, I realize my purpose has to do with the people I'm here to love and serve, and of course, that starts with me.

Let's Write

Remember to do your body and mind awareness practice (even if it's three breaths' worth) before you write. Set your timer for three minutes and write as fast as you can without censoring yourself. If three minutes isn't enough, give yourself as much time as needed and write until you're complete. You'll often notice a natural pause where the writing slows and finishes.

The Prompt

I feel purpose when _____. Try to describe all the ways you feel purpose inside you.

Room to write. . .

Feng Shui

Does purpose have a look, smell, color, or feel for you? You might write a few notes about that.

Curating your spaces to align with your purpose can mean a lot of things. Here are a few ideas to get you started. Pick one or more, or dream up your own and have fun:

- Add a faux fur throw to your bed in a favorite color

- Try a scented candle to energize a room

- String up some twinkle lights on a favorite bookshelf

- Pick your favorite paint color for an accent wall in your office

- Diffuse your favorite essential oil

Next, we'll weave your core values into the mix. With aligned purpose and values, you have powerful tools for writing your dream life.

24.

Values

I remember addressing values a long time ago when Danielle LaPorte shared a word-list exercise: "Write down 50 of your values, the ones that matter the most to you."

To save you the anticipation, our challenge was to whittle it to five. Here are mine:

Awareness
Courage
Authenticity
Positivity
Joy

I'm not sure they're the same as back then, but after years of being repeatedly told by coaches to hone it in, I came up with these five.

The more I live, the more I make clear choices about what matters to me. It's okay to change your mind. In fact, it's crucial to reevaluate, because the nature of life is change.

We get into trouble when we try to stick to old values that no longer align, or those others teach us to adopt.

At the start of life, our values come from others—parents, teachers, friends, coaches, mentors, neighbors.

No value is necessarily our own until we develop it from our lived experience or get to know ourselves better. It's amazing that other people shape those values until we wake up and realize we have a choice, that we get to explore this for ourselves, and that it doesn't have to be the same as Mom or Dad.

I remember a long-held belief about money because of something my grandparents did.

"Grandma, Grandma, we got our report cards today," I shouted, running toward the kitchen where she was simmering some pasta sauce.

"Oh yeah, let's see," she said, putting down the wooden spoon and wiping her hands on her apron.

"All As and one B," I exclaimed.

"Go grab my wallet out of my purse," she said—with less enthusiasm than I felt the moment warranted.

I was paid for perfection (for As only) and learned that if you aren't perfect, you have to work harder and achieve that to be compensated. Essentially, if I got a B, I wasn't enough.

If you get a B, you're not enough.

That worthiness thing is a doozy. This is one of the memories I do have that helped me understand who taught me what good enough means. The thing is, I made up the meaning based on her behavior. She never said, "You're not good enough." She just didn't pay for anything less than an A.

But imagine living in a worse situation.

The number of times I've read stories about people growing up in cult communities where they learn to value things others in the world judge as cruel, illegal, or worse.

We all come from an upbringing that influenced this. What was yours like? You might even make a few notes about what you made something mean. We carry those beliefs into our adulthood.

What values matter to you now? Are they different than last year?

What values will you adopt in this season of your life, and why?

These are such good questions because they can be the spotlights for writing your dream life. It takes some time to get clear about values and purpose. When you do, you have a daily, built-in alignment focus for your activities, thoughts, words, habits, and actions. You have power when you know what your values are and become unapologetic about sticking to them no matter what. You can use them for all of your boundary setting.

I asked my son recently, "What are your values? What are the core beliefs that drive you every day?"

"I don't know," he said.

"Well, that's a great place to start, with that blank slate, because you get to choose! I wasn't asked that question until well into my adult life. If someone had asked me sooner, I would've been able to get so much clearer about my life," I told him.

If you're starting with "I don't know," that's okay!

Let's Write

Remember to do your body and mind awareness practice (even if it's three breaths) before you write. Set your timer for three minutes and write as fast as you can without censoring yourself. If three minutes isn't enough, give yourself as much time as needed and write until you're complete. You'll often notice a natural pause where the writing slows and finishes.

The Prompt

1. Write down 50 words that represent what you value.

2. Cut that by half.

3. Now cut that down to five, circling those remaining words as your core values.

Next, reflect on the thoughts, habits, conversations, and behaviors you express in a day. Do they align with these five core values? You now have a new way to make choices and decisions about how you live your life.

Marry these values to your sense of purpose, and watch the sparks fly as you write your dream life into reality, fueled by that energy.

Some of the most magnetizing markers of purpose and values for abundance are gratitude, joy, love, and fun. Are you having fun yet? Let's power up the focus to these high vibrations!

Room to write. . .

_____

_____

_____

_____

_____

_____

_____

_____

_____

_____

_____

_____

_____

_____

_____

_____

_____

_____

_____

_____

_____

Feng Shui

How can you align your space with your core values? Continue your Feng Shui work from Chapter 23 and curate your space with what aligns and resonates with your values.

One day, I looked around my house at the dull white walls and thought: *I'm going to paint this room red!* That was my favorite room in the house for years.

Let's align with a little more work on gratitude next. How do you up-level gratitude vibes? Ask yourself what you appreciate.

25.

Gratitude

I'm going to put jet engines on your gratitude practice by asking: What do you appreciate?

I feel grateful for my amazing life.

I deeply appreciate the abundance flowing into my life.

Pick how you want to practice gratitude and appreciation. Choose the words that buzz in you the most, the ones that help you *feel* more. The thing about gratitude is that everyone on the planet is telling us to feel it, to be grateful for all we have, and to make that the focus of our thoughts. But many times, we're not told how to do that when we're in a bad place mentally, physically, or emotionally.

Puppies, that's how I do it.

I'm only half kidding. I truly reach for something that brings instant joy, and that's how I pull myself out of a bad day and into a higher vibe. When I'm feeling more joy, I can reach for gratitude. If I'm depressed, gratitude is a bit too far of a reach.

I don't like to "fake it till I make it," so I choose something I can't lose on. And for me, that's puppies. Real ones in person are the best choice, but if that's not possible, I'll take the ones on YouTube any day. OMG, have you found TheRockstr on Instagram yet? So funny! He never fails to make me smile, no matter how my day has been.

What's your fail-proof joy bringer? Get there first. And then, slow down, take a breath, and pay attention to the present moment you're in, looking at a funny puppy video on your phone. There is a lot to feel grateful for there:

- The deep breath of clean air you're able to take

- The ability to laugh

- The abundance that allows you to own a cellphone

We take it all for granted, don't we?

As you write your dream life, the sacred breadcrumbs light up like neon signs on your path, and it all becomes a miracle. Gratitude and appreciation are part of that scene.

But if you're not there yet, shoot for some joy before gratitude. And then latch on to joy a little more. Allow gratitude and appreciation to follow. You can appreciate your ability to feel that joy.

Let's Write

Remember to do your body and mind awareness practice (even if it's three breaths) before you write. Set your timer for three minutes and write as fast as you can without censoring yourself. If three minutes isn't enough, give yourself as much time as needed and write until you're complete. You'll often notice a natural pause where the writing slows and finishes.

The Prompt

1. The things in life that bring me joy no matter what are _____.

2. The simple things I'm most grateful for right now are _____.

3. I appreciate the ability to _____.

Room to write. . .

Feng Shui

When I practice gratitude and appreciation in my Feng Shui, I write thank-you notes. This powerful practice brings your appreciation to life and spreads it far and wide.

Write a note of appreciation and send it! You might even make that a weekly or monthly practice to regularly activate your appreciation.

Now go for joy. Joy is the most powerful manifesting energy, next to love and appreciation. More joy, please!

26.

Joy

Align with joy—three very powerful words that completely changed my life when I committed to them unapologetically.

"Why am I not happy?" That question was a wake-up call. When I realized others taught me their ways of pursuing joy and happiness—and I'd never discovered how on my own—it was life-changing.

Do I get to choose joy even though the people around me, whom I love, may not like it?

I ruminated on that thought. I felt a rotten-smelling squeeze in my solar plexus—guilt.

"Guilt is one of the only destructive emotions," my psychologist friend told me one day.

I related the choose-joy-even-if-it-upsets-others kind of guilt to duty and obligation, not right and wrong. "Well, there's healthy guilt," my psychologist friends say. "It keeps you from doing bad things."

I'm talking about the "I'm supposed to do this because I'm his daughter" kind of guilt. It's the kind you're taught to believe makes you a good person.

You're supposed to love your dad. My inner voice always reminded me that if it was family, it was obligatory, even if you were treated poorly. And I constantly felt obligatory guilt for not feeling love toward him. That guilt was a gut clench, for decades.

Those old, unhelpful messages that repeat in your mind about what a good girl does, or how she behaves, bring a destructive kind of guilt. It's good to be aware of it.

What am I doing out of obligation?

I asked myself this a lot, and learned to feel the energy of it (in my gut). The feeling was always one of constriction, never joy. Never.

How do you align with joy when you have duties and obligations? Reassess those duties, understand which were given to you by someone else (or even unconsciously by yourself), and reorganize and weed out the ones strangling your joy.

The deep breath after your weeding session should speak for itself. Give yourself permission to feel how that gut clench begins to soften and unravel. *Ahh!*

As a physical therapist and myofascial release practitioner, I attended several continuing education courses every year, my favorites being John. F. Barnes' courses. During a session on women's health, under a huge tent outside a hotel in Cape Cod, I lay on the table playing client for my partner.

We practiced releases in and around the mouth, jaw, and head. Unable to speak due to my partner's fingers pressing into my mouth, I closed my eyes as the build-up of anxiety in my chest began to frighten me. Then, all of a sudden, I took the deepest breath I've ever taken.

Whoa!

"This felt like the first breath I ever took, like the first after being born," I told my partner.

Joy feels like that—a bigger space for your soul to play, a deep relief, what you were born for.

Align with joy, and you'll write your dream life into reality faster than you can imagine.

Let's Write

Remember to do your body and mind awareness practice (even if it's three breaths' worth) before you write. Set your timer for three minutes and write as fast as you can without censoring yourself. If three minutes isn't enough, give yourself as much time as needed and write until you're complete. You'll often notice a natural pause where the writing slows and finishes.

The Prompt

Joy feels like _____ in me.

Room to write. . .

Feng Shui

The day I did my home survey, I was almost eight years post-divorce, and the list of to-dos was long. *Omg, how am I going to get all this done, or afford it?!*

I walked from room to room, listing items that needed repair or were to be thrown out, as well as the furniture or decor I didn't like or had outgrown. It was a long list.

My house was proof of my inability to speak up for my desires. I looked around for joy, and aside from baby pictures of my kids, I didn't see myself—or any joy. I saw every time I said, "Okay" to my ex, and settled on dark wood furniture, muted paint colors, or spaces with no art or expression at all. I felt the straitjacket of twenty years of compromises, trying to make a home without it actually being an expression of the grand love or joy inside me.

I threw out or gave away most of the furniture, and I slowly curated the spaces to bring me joy. The first purchase was bedroom curtains adorned with little stitched, colorful birds.

What brings you joy? Birds and nature do, in my case. I love them. I wanted them in my bedroom. Begin making a plan for bringing what you love into your spaces, whether it's color, animal prints, style, or art. Why not wake up and smile every day?

To really get you aligned with the magnetic energy that creates everything you want and want to feel, let's continue with love, a universal force of a dream life.

27.

Love

While writing this book, I thought: *Who are you to talk about love?*

I asked for a divorce after 20 years of marriage. I'm not sure I had a clue. But the longer I moved toward the feeling of love just to feel it, without attaching it to anything anyone was supposed to give me, the more wonderful the *aha* moments became.

And then an answer: *You are a poet who has dedicated her life to awareness. You are the perfect person to write about love.*

I'm thinking you, dear reader, are a perfect person to write about love, too. Because this world needs your story (all of our stories) about it.

I remember one afternoon of ruminating about my relationship with my dad. My moments then were about forgiveness:

What if I could let go of everything I'm mad, sad, or disappointed about and just forgive him? He was doing the best he could with what he had at the time. Hurt people hurt people.

I read *Radical Forgiveness,* among other books on the topic. I learned about the process from healer friends. I touched the place in me that knew: *Forgiveness is for **you**, not them. Carrying anger around about someone else will only poison you.*

I was ready.

Rather than doing anything in particular, I just let go of all my thoughts. I brought my mind into a peaceful space, watched the bright green leaves on the trees outside giggle in the summer breeze, and felt the gratitude for being alive.

And forgiveness came—a wave of love. It felt like what unconditional love should feel like: powerful and overwhelming.

"I love you dad," I whispered. "I'm good. Thank you for helping me be who I was meant to be in this world."

When you can love someone you once despised, it's transformational. Somehow, we feel like forgiveness is letting the person off the hook for their abysmal behavior. But when it comes, that unconditional love wave, spreading through your heart and every cell in your body, you know it's not about that. The medicine you've given yourself is better than any you've ever given yourself before.

Align with love.

What's a moment where you felt love as an energy rather than a feeling of adoration toward someone? Where was it in your body? How did that feel? Have you ever felt love as a palpable feeling? It's okay if you're not sure. It's fun to be curious.

The biggest question I ask myself about love is: *How can you give that to yourself today?*

I know when I feel love inside, then I can give it away. When I bring it to me, I can bring it to the world.

Let's Write

Remember to do your body and mind awareness practice (even if it's three breaths' worth) before you write. Set your timer for three minutes and write as fast as you can without censoring yourself. If three minutes isn't enough, give yourself as much time as needed and write until you're complete. You'll often notice a natural pause where the writing slows and finishes.

The Prompt

Love feels like _____ in me.

Room to write. . .

Feng Shui

I've been taking a course called The Love Camp from. . .from Dana Claudat. She uses art to connect with love and self-love. I love the meditative aspect of art. My friend Jean Voice Dart, the lead author of *Expressive Arts,* knows this well, too. She and her expert cast of co-authors gifted us a book full of ways to connect through art.

Today, choose an art project and play. It could be doodling, drawing, painting, dancing, singing, or any other activity that lets you express and connect with your essence. I love art journaling. I often grab magazines, markers, and stickers to create art journal pages for a little variety from my usual journaling.

And, speaking of fun, why don't we remember that, too? Because if we're not having some fun on this Earth school, then what's it all for?

28.

Fun

"If we're not having fun in this life, then I don't know what we're doing here," I said to a friend.

"Truth," she replied.

I wonder how long that will last. I doubted my ability to keep focused on my mantra about fun. My guess was: *Not long.*

We lose our childlike wonder and connection to fun so quickly in life, it seems. We're conditioned to "adult" and to our responsibilities so fast. Nobody teaches us how to keep having fun while we're doing that.

We quickly fall back into patterns of negative focus. We get so serious so quickly that we forget something important. We're all going to die.

If we can't let go and have fun on this ride, I'm not sure what we're doing here.

Do you remember when you were having so much fun as a kid, and a voice boomed, "Be quiet!" Do you remember a version that went something like, "Go to your room if you're going to do that!"

Or maybe, "You're being too loud. Quiet down! Find somewhere else to make all that racket!"

In other words, your fun wasn't right, appropriate, or allowed. It was too loud, too much. It was sometimes bad or had consequences. And you learned to stay quiet and have less fun.

Bummer.

This makes me a little sad. Some of the grown-ups around me had a low tolerance for fun. That translated over to me learning that the way to behave in the world was "quiet," "alone," and "cautious."

I know families that dance and sing together. I rarely remember adults dancing, singing, or listening to music in my family homes, except for my grandparents' 50th anniversary, when we danced to a DJ.

I know there are quiet ways to have fun, but I'm talking about the singing and dancing that were often loud, boisterous fun! And when those expressions aren't met with approval, we learn they're wrong. We create that belief. Some of us live our entire lives taking life way too seriously and then teach others through our behavior. We forget how to play. And then we model that for our kids.

During an adult birthday celebration at our house one hot July, I pulled out water balloons for the kids. And then a couple of the adults and I got involved. I will never forget the look on my son's face (he may have been seven or eight at the time) when he saw me running around throwing water balloons and shouted, "That's my mom!"

In the middle of play, creativity and imagination produce dreams. It's the in-the-moment focus with a sprinkle of joy (extremely powerful energy) that acts as a magnet for more joy energy and a life you desire.

It's time to have more fun. And not fun that's necessarily productive, but fun for fun's sake, for the joy of it, for the exploration.

Fun moments can be different for different people. For me, connecting with nature on a long walk in the woods is fun and relaxing. For a different kind of fun, I'll look for an open-mic event where I can share time with my poet friends. I love comedy specials on Netflix. And playing a board game with my family and talking about life around the table is also fun! Water balloon fights? Definitely fun.

When you think about having fun, how does that feel to you? What are the qualities that make that moment or experience feel fun? What makes you smile or laugh?

"When I'm having fun, I forget about what I look and sound like, and most of the time, I'm laughing. I'm engaged in the moment and grounded in joy, so all the other worries of life dissipate," I told my friend.

"I always feel my fun when the sides of my mouth start to hurt from the smiles and laughter," she replied.

"Yes! It's like nothing else exists. You're so powerfully in joy. It's that laugh that creates the unintended snort!"

"Ha! Yes. We did this laughter yoga thing the other day, and I almost peed my pants; it was so fun."

Yeah, what about those kinds of moments? Why aren't we purposefully creating our day to lean into that more often? Who says we can't work and have fun at the same time?

And when you have fun, you're practicing the energy of creation, love, joy, and happiness. It's badass manifesting energy!

Let's Write

Remember to do your body and mind awareness practice (even if it's three breaths' worth) before you write. Set your timer for three minutes and write as fast as you can without censoring yourself. If three minutes isn't enough, give yourself as much time as needed and write until you're complete. You'll often notice a natural pause where the writing slows and finishes.

The Prompt

When I'm having fun, I feel _____.

Room to write. . .

_____

_____

_____

_____

_____

_____

_____

_____

_____

_____

_____

_____

_____

_____

_____

_____

_____

_____

_____

Feng Shui

Make cleaning fun!

As a mom who carried resentment toward cleaning and doing laundry for many years, I can tell you that when you make cleaning fun, everything will change in your home. First of all, your house will stay cleaner, but the energy in your home will vibrate higher from the simple fact that you are vibrating at a higher frequency.

Mostly, this is an attitude adjustment. Mentally, when I realized the power of cleaning in my Feng Shui practice, it was no longer a have-to. It became a want-to. I felt better in clean, clear, curated spaces. I wanted to live in them. Living in clean spaces is enjoyable; it helps you physically, mentally, and emotionally, but also creatively.

How to make cleaning fun:

- Put on music you love.

- Listen to Esther Hicks' Law of Attraction rants while you clean.

- Imagine having magical powers as you clean—every surface becomes part of attracting abundance.

- Use scents you love (I use peppermint essential oil and a wonderful blend from DoTerra called Serenity in my cleaning sprays).

- Invest in new, more powerful cleaning tools. I purchased a steam cleaner for small surfaces like the bathrooms, and a new, lighter weight Dyson that I could manage on the stairs. Now I can't wait to use my cool tools!

Okay, amazing readers, we've completed the Write to Align section, and we're joyfully headed toward Write to Manifest. But heads up: You've already primed the pump with the last several prompts. Hopefully, you're feeling the energy of gratitude, love, joy, and fun! These are powerful energies.

With awareness, you have a choice, even on a bad day, to pivot to any feeling you prefer. You can focus on what's good and the feelings you want more of at any moment. This isn't to avoid the emotions; it's to consciously choose the path and what energy you want to practice in that moment.

The energy you're feeling and practicing in the moment is the life you're living and what you'll attract more of.

It's the now moment, and what you do with it that matters.

What will you choose to think, feel, write, and manifest?

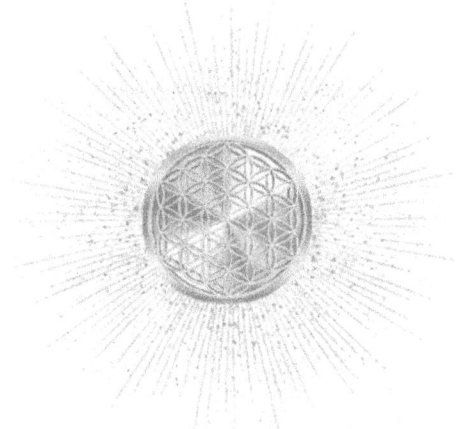

Part 4

Write to Manifest
(Live in Joy)

I'm so excited you've made it to this part of the book. This is where magic happens. This is where you write your life into existence with the power of energy and intention. This is where you go beyond your gratitude list and declare your desires in a way that helps you experience them.

This is the magic fairy dust, the magic wand, the secret to it all, the practice of the master manifestors. Are you living in joy today?

An Ode to My Writer Friends
By Laura Di Franco

I scratch my dreams
All the most important things
Down into the sacred fibers
Of my paper

The blank canvas receives
Thoughts, desires, imaginings
Chunks of heart and soul
And it's alchemy

I watch as my dream life arrives
Through carefully curated lines
One after another
Stopping time

Magic occurs in these little curves
No matter if they're seasoned
With tears or smiles
It's a spell

I cast them wildly sometimes
And others flow with purpose so intense
They singe the edges of reality
Leaving ashes

Carried away by sweet spring breezes
I realize I created exactly
What I asked for. . .
These are manifesting pages!

So I pause and breathe
Deep inspiration, trust, and joy
Rise to the surface
And out of my pen

I send it all up as my ask
I know it's given, and then. . .
All that remains to do
Is bask.

It's time to write!

29.

What You're Good At

When you're good at something, you know it. It's easy. It's fun. It feels like what you were put here to do.

Doing what you're good at infuses you with a feeling of joy and confidence. It's a knowing feeling combined with other good feelings. It might even be as strong as faith.

There was an exercise in one of Kyle Cease's books *(I Hope I Screwed This Up)* that asked us to write down 50 things we were good at. *Whoa, 50?* I struggled but completed the exercise. I loved the positive focus.

So, take a break now and do that homework if it turns you on. It's a great exercise. Anything you feel good at—small, medium, or large—counts. Making a great cup of coffee is one of mine! Ever had bulletproof coffee with Kerrygold whipped butter? Oh my.

What you're good at could come from things you've practiced. Maybe you started with some natural talent, but with practice, you honed your skills and became really good at it.

When my son and I trained in Taekwondo, we started with our white belts. I could do a few kicks in the beginning, being the lifelong athlete I was at the time. But after six years of practice and our black belt exam, I could perform an axe kick that would've won an award. Or at least I thought so!

I was good at those kicks after a while. It felt good. Being in my body and performing them felt great. I got to the point where I competed in Poomsae (forms) and won awards in my age category.

When you're ready to write your dream life, lean on what you know about yourself and what you can do, even if it's making that great cup of coffee. It's the confidence and joy you're after—the feeling. When you're faced with a task you don't know as well, remind yourself that you've learned new things before and become great at them.

Your list of things you're good at might even include an inspired idea for something new, or a solution to a problem you currently have. Use those skills you're good at and apply them to the new problem. See what happens.

When you're doing something you're good at, you feel good about yourself, it boosts your self-esteem, and the energy is higher-vibe. This is the idea.

So that list of 50 is a start!

Let's add to it.

Let's Write

Remember to do your body and mind awareness practice (even if it's three breaths' worth) before you write. Set your timer for three minutes and write as fast as you can without censoring yourself. If three minutes isn't enough, give yourself as much time as needed and write until you're complete. You'll often notice a natural pause where the writing slows and finishes.

The Prompt

Choose one thing you love to do so much that you lose track of time. Something you feel good at. Share a story about it here with every detail. Help us see, taste, smell, feel, and hear it.

Room to write. . .

Feng Shui

As I practice Feng Shui more and more, I always look for ways to align my spaces with all the things I love, and to bring ease into my life. When my home helps me feel at ease, I can do all the things I do for my family and for the world better. I'm clearer, more focused, and my vibration is higher when my home is functional.

Where do you need more organization in your home to help bring ease to your daily life?

Here are some projects to think about. When you organize a physical space, remember to:

1. Take everything out.

2. Clean with a natural cleaning spray.

3. Throw out anything that's junk, never used, or that doesn't serve you anymore.

4. Put everything back in a neat, organized fashion.

Pick one (or more) projects to Feng Shui:

- Organize your kitchen cupboards/pantry for easy access to everything you need.

- Organize your email inbox with folders that make it easy to find important messages.

- Organize your linen closet.

- Organize your refrigerator.

- Organize your filing cabinet (home or office).

- Organize your business systems into folders of operating procedures.

- Organize that junk drawer!

Small or large, these projects will bring a sense of calm and ease to your day. The more, the better! Organized spaces lend themselves to increased productivity. What you can accomplish becomes more limitless.

If you're like me, you may run from one accomplishment to another, rarely slowing down to notice what goals you've met. Let's manifest by slowing down to celebrate what you've already done.

30.

What You've Accomplished

Accomplishments are often overlooked when they're complete because you move on to the next too rapidly. So, we're going to pause in the energy of accomplishment for a moment and really bask.

Imagine something you've accomplished. Spend some time with this. Take a few deep breaths and see what comes to mind. Did you allow yourself any moment of celebration?

As you scan your past, maybe there was a time when you learned to drive, graduated from college, took your first trip without a chaperone, or earned an A on that test. Maybe you landed a new job, wrote your first article, or published a book.

I remember completing my black belt exam, getting a compliment on a meal I made for the family, teaching my dog how to roll over, getting married, getting divorced, going out of the country by myself for the first time, juggling a soccer ball on my foot, learning that axe kick, and giving birth twice (okay that should be at the top of the accomplishment list).

So many defining moments over a lifetime, right?

But think of the *energy* you experienced in the moment of accomplishment. What was the feeling?

When you felt happy, joyful, encouraged, empowered, accomplished, or proud, what did you feel in your body? What was the scene, and how did it play out? Did others have to be present to acknowledge that accomplishment? Could you feel it by yourself? Reflect for a few moments and feel it now. Breathe.

A month or so after the black belt exam, my son (11 at the time) and I held a party for our classmates, family, and friends. Nobody in our school had done that before. *Nobody thought to celebrate?*

I questioned it at first: *Maybe we're not supposed to celebrate?*

I worried I was doing it wrong.

I'm laughing at that today. Celebration is one of the most powerful manifesting energies there is!

In May of 2025, my company celebrated 100 published book titles with an all-day online party. My intent was the same: to pause the train long enough to bask in the energy of the accomplishment, in that joy and celebration.

Ooh, you guys, celebration energy is powerful. Don't miss an opportunity to celebrate.

And when it comes to others' accomplishments, please recognize that even though the success isn't directly yours, it's an energy you can practice so that it feels like it is. So, when your friends are celebrating, don't miss a juicy morsel of it. Help plan that party! You'll be living in the energy, which is a powerful magnet for that exact energy to be drawn to you!

This is so important in entrepreneurship as we look around at people doing all the things and wonder: *When is it my turn?*

Don't fall for that self-sabotage. Grab on to your friends' celebrations and help them, and you'll be in the energy for yourself, too.

Let's Write

Remember to do your body and mind awareness practice (even if it's three breaths' worth) before you write. Set your timer for three minutes and write as fast as you can without censoring yourself. If three minutes isn't enough, give yourself as much time as needed and write until you're complete. You'll often notice a natural pause where the writing slows and finishes.

The Prompt

Today I celebrate _____.

Note: Celebration can be for things small, medium, or large. Don't let the idea that it has to be some huge accomplishment prevent you from celebrating. Sometimes just getting up in the morning is worth a celebration!

Room to write. . .

_____

_____

_____

_____

_____

_____

_____

_____

_____

_____

_____

_____

_____

_____

_____

_____

_____

_____

_____

_____

Feng Shui

If you look at the Bagua map, remember you have a legacy area of your home (or room) at left center of the space. This is a wonderful place to celebrate. The legacy area of your home is great for celebrating your heritage, family, and accomplishments. Do you have a degree you never framed, or a photo of you graduating? One of my favorite photos is of my son and me on black belt exam day. But I didn't have that displayed for a long time.

The trick to curating your spaces for celebration is to bring that energy to the forefront by using decor that reminds you of it.

In my office, I have a section of one wall where I display photos, cards from friends, little trinkets, good-luck charms, or inspirational messages. You can get cool magnetic strips with colorful magnets, or a magnetic whiteboard for your office to display different things that help you celebrate.

Next, we'll live our ideal day now. This journaling practice changed my life.

31.

The Ideal Day

"Write out your ideal morning in every detail. Make sure to make us feel, taste, hear, smell, and see it. If there were no obstacles and unlimited resources, what would your ideal, perfect day look like?"

I remember loving this writing prompt from one of my coaches. It was the beginning of a journaling technique I've recently come to know as "pray rain" in my Feng Shui class. It's writing the scene like you're living it in the moment.

I remember my ideal morning was a scene in a farmhouse in front of a huge fireplace, sitting on a fuzzy white rug with a handsome man sharing a deep conversation. Today, I can still see the living room and the glow of the fire. The man, not so much. The wonderful feeling came from the safe, cozy, warm space and the time I had to bask.

We're after that kind of feeling with this journaling technique. It's transformational because of the science that tells us imagining something and living it are the same experience for the brain. That means the same manifesting energy.

Writing as if you're living it now is a powerful manifesting tool. The trick is getting into the energy and vibration of the vision, like you're living the scene. Your brain doesn't know the difference between the actual scene and the imagined one. You set yourself up for success when you visualize it.

Writing it down is a bit trickier because we tend to add words that carry a lack vibration. We think we're writing it the right way, but we actually introduce doubt into the vibration.

Instead of saying, "I'm so happy and grateful now that _____," we type words like, "What I truly want right now is _____." Using words like *want, desire, wish, hope,* or negative words like *pain-free,* focuses on the lower-vibration word, rather than the desired outcome.

"What's the feeling when there is no pain in your body?" my coach asked. "Feel and describe it—write those words. Try not to use the word *pain* at all."

Oh, that's tough, I thought. *How can I write it if I don't have it yet?*

And that's the exact secret of this: writing, feeling, and being it before you have the real manifestation of it. Your ideal day *can* be written in a 100% positive, living-it-now kind of way. And there are some subtle shifts to pay attention to.

Example:

Instead of: "I'll wake up in the morning to watch the sunrise, grab my notebook and pen, and sip my dark roast as the light pierces through the leaves."

Write: "Waking in the morning is incredible. The sunrise light pierces the leaves and casts a golden glow everywhere. As I taste the first sip of my espresso, I feel so much peace. I'm ready to write."

The simple shift here is changing "I'll (I will)" to "waking" and creating an active version of the scene as I experience it in my body and mind's eye.

When you create your ideal day, envision and feel the scene, then write as you feel.

Let's Write

Remember to do your body and mind awareness practice (even if it's three breaths' worth) before you write. Set your timer for three minutes and write as fast as you can without censoring yourself. If three minutes isn't enough, give yourself as much time as needed and write until you're complete. You'll often notice a natural pause where the writing slows and finishes.

The Prompt

Write out your ideal morning, including every juicy detail. Make sure to envision and feel as you write. Continue with the entire ideal day. Take as much time as you need!

Another version for my entrepreneur friends: I love doing this same exercise for my life and business. Think big vision here. In your manifested reality of the empire you've built, how is that day going? What are you doing? Who are you talking to? What team is around you? This is one of my new New Year journaling exercises, and it's powerful.

Room to write. . .

Feng Shui

There are some Feng Shui activities I do on a regular basis (aside from normal cleaning), which I've found add magnetism to my life and business. Dana taught them to us in her School of Intention. Here's my personal list. Try them out!

- Clean the front door with warm, soapy, peppermint-essential-oil-infused water.

- Clean the stovetop.

- Curate my corners with a pinch of cinnamon.

- Add a tiny bit of Manuka honey to my coffee.

- Clean my office desk with thieves cleaning spray and light my gold glitter-sparkle candle during my Zooms.

Now, create your own list!

So, what about manifesting people into your life? Let's talk about curating the inner circle that helps you live your dream life next.

32.

The Perfect Relationship

There's no perfect relationship. If you're starting from a place that looks a lot like a Disney movie, pause. Understand what you were taught about relationships.

I listened to Dana Claudat talk about our "love story" in her Love Camp workshop, and I paused the video and thought about mine.

It's really pretty simple. I get it. The entire first part of my life, I pursued worthiness. I wasn't pretty or smart enough to be worthy of love from a man. So, if you're not enough, then. . .

I felt sad thinking about this at first, and my story included blaming my dad for pretty much everything I felt. My parents divorced when I was eight. My dad cheated on my mom. Love was messed up. It wasn't about devotion, adoration, or commitment (the things I deeply desired). I'm not even really sure what it was about.

I pivoted quickly after listening for a few more minutes.

I forgive my dad. He was—both my parents were—just working with the awareness and resources they had at the time. What that lifelong pursuit did for me was help me be the amazing woman I am today, with this gigantic mission to help the world experience what's possible in terms of healing. I'm grateful.

I've been down this thought process road many times. But when Dana called this our "love story," something clicked. I remember someone talking about our "money story" and realized that everything we think we have difficulty with comes from some old, unhelpful story we're still telling ourselves—sometimes decades later.

The self-sabotaging bullshit can be fierce. But we're more powerful inside the awareness we've been cultivating and can quickly turn around even the most longstanding, ingrained thoughts and beliefs.

Relationships—it's one of the most profound topics that exists. What's your "love story"? What story have you told yourself over the years about relationships and your part in them? What thoughts or beliefs have you lived (probably for decades)? It's time to raise awareness of those stories and focus more on the life you're living in this moment, which is anything you desire.

This may take a few minutes of meditation, contemplation, reflection, and journaling. So do that now before you get to manifesting. There may be a little Feng Shui to do on the topic first!

What's your new relationship story going to be? The new love story? The story of the inner circle of support you have in your life and business?

In the Law of Attraction, you know how we're told not to worry about the how? In other words, let the Universe deliver in whatever magical way it does, and your job is to imagine in feeling and vibration language. When you get too specific, it tends to slow the manifesting train down.

I highly suggest considering that before you imagine your perfect relationship, especially if you're hoping to meet someone you haven't met yet.

What is the scene (just like your ideal day) *of feelings* in that scenario? When a relationship is going really well, what's being said, what are you doing together, and how do you feel as these moments occur? More importantly, what feelings are you experiencing in those moments that make it perfect? That's the energy we can practice, which means we can manifest more of it.

Let the feelings direct your journaling.

Let's Write

Remember to do your body and mind awareness practice (even if it's three breaths' worth) before you write. Set your timer for three minutes and write as fast as you can without censoring yourself. If three minutes isn't enough, give yourself as much time as needed and write until you're complete. You'll often notice a natural pause where the writing slows and finishes.

The Prompt

Write a scene (like your ideal day) of a perfect day with your beloved. No rules about this "relationship." This can be a partner/lover, friend, family member, new acquaintance, client, or business partner. What's the scene in that dream relationship? Maybe it's simply the relationship with yourself!

Let us be a fly on the wall.

Room to write. . .

_____

_____

_____

_____

_____

_____

_____

_____

_____

_____

_____

_____

_____

_____

_____

_____

_____

_____

_____

_____

_____

Feng Shui

Is there space in your life for a relationship? Maybe it's time to Feng Shui your bedroom and include two nightstands.

Have you practiced self-love? Maybe curate that feeling inside first, today.

Are you in love with yourself first? Or is self-sabotage creeping into your mind again?

These are hard questions most of us tackle last on this journey.

It doesn't matter whether I desired a husband or a badass business collaboration partner; when I learned to love myself and practice the energy of worthiness, gratitude, adoration, and love inside me, more of that came my way. I'll practice this one forever. Some days I'm really great at it!

Here's another thing that happens when you practice: What doesn't serve naturally drops away.

I made a vow to the Universe recently: *If this relationship isn't the right one for me, make it plainly clear and take care of it for me.*

I looked back on my past relationships, my broken engagement, my one marriage, and all the times I tried (hard) to be everything so that they'd love me—and I got tired of that nonsense. I knew I had to learn the lesson. It wouldn't matter if I broke off another relationship; someone else would come along to teach me the lesson again.

But what is this lesson? I may have included the F-word in that thought.

And you know the lesson, right? It's *you* who must change. The focus and the vibration in you come first, not any outward fixing of someone else. In the case of mental, emotional, or physical abuse, get the heck out of the environment.

But if you love someone who treats you well, but who has some things to work on, guess what? So do you. And this is where I am with my love relationship today.

My practice is to focus on the energy I desire and curate it in me (and in my spaces) without anyone else in the picture, so I manifest more of it. I've surrendered the *how* of that, how the Universe will bring what I desire to me.

It could be my partner who brings that to me. It could be a new friend. It could be a new business relationship or partner.

Try creating spaces you love in your home. Go back to a few of the prior chapters for ideas.

Speaking of business partners, let's talk about that dream job or career next!

33.

The Ideal Job or Career

"Laura, are you ready?"

"Yep, I'm coming."

I tucked the pink button-down shirt into my khaki pants and took a deep breath. *I hope it's good,* I thought as I entered my boss's office. It was performance appraisal day. I was due for that three percent cost-of-living increase, and I deserved every penny.

As I sat with Michelle as she shared the checklist of performance items, and explained how she'd marked each with her feedback, I instantly felt not-good-enough.

I saw the "2%" at the bottom of the page and was deaf to the feedback. *I'm not good enough.*

It was my first job after my internship and graduation from physical therapy school. My perfectionism was intense, and this was such a hit to my ego that I felt nauseous.

Later in my career, as the manager of an outpatient clinic, I was demoted after standing up for one of our best employees with upper management. My boss sent me to work in two other clinics and asked me to split my time while doubling my commute.

While this was one of those "everything happens for you" scenarios I can talk about positively now, the job wasn't ideal. Back then, I didn't even ask myself what my dream job would look like. I was just happy to have a job I loved that brought in a good salary and offered great healthcare benefits.

After the demotion, I started to love the job less. Not to mention one of the bosses in the two clinics swore at his employees as a regular management strategy. *If doing what's right means more of this kind of pain, it'll never be worth working for a boss again.*

Then I pictured working for myself and about my dream physical therapy career: one I owned. There are a couple more steps in my journey to becoming my own boss for real, but the point of this is a question I should've asked in the beginning:

What does the ideal, dream job or career look, taste, feel, sound, and smell like?

They should teach "Write Your Dream Job" courses to college students, where we practice the energy, intention, and vibration of an incredibly purposeful and fulfilling career, then write down the details of it.

It's not too late, though, no matter what stage you're in. You might be in a transition. You might be burning out in your current job. You might be forced to get a job because of a divorce, death, or other circumstances. So why not write that career into reality right now?

For those of you already in your dream job or career, have you ever played with the question: How could this be better?

When we hit our upper limit, we often take our foot off the gas pedal and wallow in "contentment." What else is possible? If there were absolutely no limits to your resources, what would you do?

Let's Write

Remember to do your body and mind awareness practice (even if it's three breaths' worth) before you write. Set your timer for three minutes and write as fast as you can without censoring yourself. If three minutes isn't enough, give yourself as much time as needed and write until you're complete. You'll often notice a natural pause where the writing slows and finishes.

The Prompt

Write a scene (like your ideal day) of your perfect job, career, or purposeful endeavor. No rules. Help us be a fly on the wall in that scenario. Add every detail, conversation, and specific emotion or feeling.

Room to write. . .

_____

_____

_____

_____

_____

_____

_____

_____

_____

_____

_____

_____

_____

_____

_____

_____

_____

_____

_____

_____

_____

_____

Feng Shui

Dress the part and Feng Shui your wardrobe to fit the job or career you want.

I've worked with two stylists over my years in business. The first hire was because I started stepping onto stages and wanted to feel the same on the outside as I did on the inside—confident and excited! Over the years, my goals changed and what I realized is that she was dressing me for a picture that wasn't mine; it was hers. So, I had to figure out how to become more me.

It wasn't until my daughter became a young adult and dove into fashion that I realized I had no style.

"No, Mom," she said, watching me look at myself in the mirror one day.

"What's wrong with this?" I retorted.

"It doesn't go together," she said.

Ugh, I have no sense of style.

I was used to purchasing comfortable clothes (nothing wrong with that) that I liked, but nothing felt like it went together or formed any kind of overall style.

I noticed that as I branded my business, I craved having a style to my wardrobe.

What's your style?

Activity: Do a closet overhaul (I do this a couple of times a year). Throw out what you haven't worn in an entire year. Clear some space, and then you can begin to curate a wardrobe that helps you feel like yourself.

Feeling great in your clothes is living your dream life. It's the full, external expression of your uniqueness. It matters!

On another topic that matters, let's dive into your spiritual support next, one foundation of your practice.

34.

Spiritual Support

"I'm spiritual, not religious," I said to my networking partner, instantly second-guessing whether I offended them by saying it.

What if they are religious? I wondered, taking a deep breath at the same time.

They have to love you, the whole you, and if they don't, well, so be it.

Over my lifetime, conforming to be liked, noticed, valued, and worthy has been a pattern. I broke it a decade ago, but notice remnants of old, bad habits surfacing now and again when I'm in a triggering situation.

"Responding rather than reacting is a ninja move," I told my daughter one day. This is absolutely one of the only ways you can feel in control over your life.

So much of my spiritual journey has been about reclaiming my worth and sovereignty, and living in my truth, no matter what. Every single spiritual resource, support, idea, friend, or course helped me get to the root: You were born, so you're worthy. And from that grounded, centered, empowered place, I moved forth in the world and pursued purpose and joy.

When you write your dream life, don't forget to write in this kind of support, this knowing, and this practice. A spiritual life is a daily, moment-by-moment practice. Your moments are the ritual. Your faith in something—that bigger energy or presence—carries you in the worst possible moments.

What do you believe in?

"Do you believe in something bigger than you?" I asked my son one day.

"I don't know," he replied.

OMG, I failed, I thought. *I haven't introduced him to the most important aspect of life there is: his belief in something bigger.*

My journey pushed me into spiritual practices in my 20s. I'm grateful for that. Now, five years post-COVID, I watch my 20-something children navigate life with no foundation to help them through it, and I'm afraid.

What if they never feel their purpose? What if this world takes them down and they don't survive it?

They've had me as a model, I remember.

They've watched you navigate it. They're learning from your model.

I exhale, noticing I'd been holding my breath longer than I realized.

They will be on a path that is specifically for them. You're good. You're a good mom, and you've done a great job.

I like that voice. I've learned to listen to my inner wisdom more than my inner critic, and if it weren't for understanding and discerning between those voices, I wouldn't have much of a spiritual foundation at all. I think that *is* the spiritual path—the learning of your own soul's voice, the inner wisdom, the knowing, the voice of that bigger Source energy.

So, let's write and practice now. Every single time you write words on the page, take advantage of this amazing opportunity to create a spiritual experience. You're living it as you write.

Let's Write

Remember to do your body and mind awareness practice (even if it's three breaths' worth) before you write. Set your timer for three minutes and write as fast as you can without censoring yourself. If three minutes isn't enough, give yourself as much time as needed and write until you're complete. You'll often notice a natural pause where the writing slows and finishes.

The Prompt

I love the feeling of spirit in me. It feels like _____.

Room to write. . .

Feng Shui

What aspects of your spaces and/or daily routine support your spiritual beliefs?

My suggestion for you is to start (or enhance) a meditation practice. Essentially, get still and quiet, in whatever form you can and that works for you—even if it's five minutes a day. This stillness is the space from which all messages from that bigger place move through.

This is helping to Feng Shui your mind. It's crucial.

As we figure out our spiritual life, we wander toward our purpose. After knowing "I was born, so I'm worthy," I had a chance to ask another question: What is my highest purpose in this life? Whoa, what an incredible question.

My highest purpose?

Go back to review Chapter 23 before moving on. Really understand the idea of purpose, and then let's take this further.

35.

Your Highest Purpose

"You don't have an assigned purpose in this life. You give the meaning to your purpose."

I admit, when I first heard my teacher say this, I was like, *WTF are you talking about; isn't everyone born with a certain purpose?*

I quickly realized it's not a specific topic, a certain cause, or anything like that at all. It's about the feeling of joy inside. I've felt joy inside for many reasons over many decades, and it's changed over time!

What if the purpose you think you're born with—the one you follow and find a career in—changes? Does that mean you no longer have a purpose? No, it means you get to change your mind and follow your joy.

Purpose is not one task or job you must fulfill. Nobody is holding you to a certain performance here. Purpose, in this moment, might have a face or a name, or even just a feeling.

But what about a *higher* calling or purpose? Is this the same idea?

Writing my dream life has meant living in my aligned purpose (joy) every day. When I imagine my higher purpose, knowing I'm worthy because I was born, the only job I have left is to find joy.

This sounds so simple. Some days it feels impossible. Every day is a chance to detach from the outcome and understand it's all *for* us.

My higher purpose always works itself out with and for me. It's a matter of whether I'm paying attention or not. Understanding this kind of daily awareness and practice (more like a discipline) is a game-changer. This level of awareness is one of my strongest values, a foundation for every other value I follow.

When I remember nothing is good or bad, and that every single thing is happening for me, I pause, breathe, reframe, shift my vibration, and attract something different.

The skill is remembering.

Higher purpose has to do with more than what we can see, hear, taste, and touch right now. It's in small moments when I ask myself: *What will your future self be happy you did?*

Living in higher purpose requires surrender, acceptance, and detachment—fierce awareness. I'm not sure I make it there every day, but I like the feeling when I do, so I practice getting there as often as possible.

When do you feel you're in a higher calling of purpose? What does that feel like?

We now have an opportunity to write this into reality.

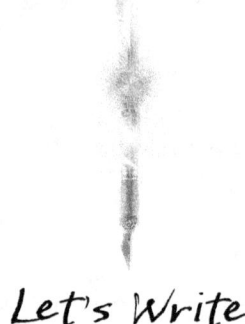

Let's Write

Remember to do your body and mind awareness practice (even if it's three breaths' worth) before you write. Set your timer for three minutes and write as fast as you can without censoring yourself. If three minutes isn't enough, give yourself as much time as needed and write until you're complete. You'll often notice a natural pause where the writing slows and finishes.

The Prompt

When I feel a higher purpose, _____.

Room to write. . .

_____

_____

_____

_____

_____

_____

_____

_____

_____

_____

_____

_____

_____

_____

_____

_____

_____

_____

_____

_____

_____

Feng Shui

Knowing the higher purpose of joy created an urge in me to make every day an opportunity to pursue it, no matter what was happening.

Every morning as I feel myself waking up, I pause to gaze at the back of my eyelids before I move. I enjoy a few moments to notice that quiet space and bring gratitude in to start my day.

Create a mantra, ritual, meditation, or activity for yourself that points you to *your* higher purpose. It's important to craft this uniquely for you. Take pieces of the things you've learned and decide on something you'll try today.

Living in a higher purpose naturally breeds authentic leaders. If you find yourself building community without trying, it probably means you're leading authentically, whether you know it or not. Let's flow into that kind of leadership next, and how it might help you live your dream life.

36.

Servant Leadership

"Servant leadership is a philosophy and style of leadership where the leader's primary goal is to serve and prioritize the needs, growth, and well-being of their team members (community) and the organization." ~ Google definition

Servant leadership comes after and with radical self-care, and shouldn't prioritize others before your own health. If you're living your dream life, you're healthy, wealthy, and energized every day, and service comes from overflow. That's the foundation of reaching the definition above.

When my cup overflows and there's plenty to give without draining the cup, I lead well (both myself and others).

You may not feel like leadership is something you need for a dream life, but what if it's just being a leader of your own life—that sovereignty? Full worthiness at the helm of your ship, steering toward the lighthouse of joy might be the goal. You have an opportunity to lead in this way, every day, or not. Where are you leading your own life?

Self-care and self-love are how you lead yourself. They're the modalities that help you lead others effectively.

Only there, in that place of full, healthy, overflowing empowerment, will you lead others in a way that changes the world for good, if leading others is your goal.

What's your version of leadership? What does that look and feel like? There's no one picture or rule about how this looks. The idea is to create your own from a foundation of awareness, joy, and genuine desire to make the world a better place.

I serve myself first. I am my community and priority. Once I am taken care of in the best way, I can move into the world with my business, mission, and vision, and support everyone I love and serve. And, no, I don't get this perfect every day. I aim toward it with intention.

My dream life is a daily ritual of this feeling—and definitely a practice of getting to it when I'm not quite there.

Knowing what that kind of leadership tastes, smells, and feels like is the beginning of living it. Writing those things down (while you feel them) creates it in that moment.

We have a huge opportunity to manifest authentic leadership and community building, starting with ourselves.

Let's do it.

Let's Write

Remember to do your body and mind awareness practice (even if it's three breaths' worth) before you write. Set your timer for three minutes and write as fast as you can without censoring yourself. If three minutes isn't enough, give yourself as much time as needed and write until you're complete. You'll often notice a natural pause where the writing slows and finishes.

The Prompt

To lead myself every day in a way that feels blissful, I _____.

Room to write. . .

Feng Shui

Choose one self-care activity that helps clear your energy field today. This is the most powerful Feng Shui there is!

Here are some ideas:

- Breathwork

- Smudge yourself with Palo Santo

- Sound healing

- Journaling

- Take an Epsom salt and essential oil bath

Leaders tend to be visionaries. Do you identify as either? Let's play with what it means to be a visionary, even if it just means doing that for your own amazing life.

37.

Visionary Alien Dreams

"I call you one of my visionary alien badasses," I said to a colleague over Zoom.

"You've got other-level dreams, and you're making them happen! Your mind runs at 150 mph, and you take a lot of action. You have a million ideas a minute. You take risks to make your dream life happen. You're not afraid of failure, and when something doesn't work, you treat it as a lesson learned and wake up the next day to start again."

She nodded her head, smiled, and replied, "And it's hard being her some days."

That's when I nodded with full-body resonance and said, "And that's why we need each other. When you play in the sandbox with a community that holds you accountable to your mindset and big vision, you become unstoppable. That's what I want to do for each other."

My Brave Healer Dream Program for authors was born of this powerful energy of collaboration and community, from a selfish need to stop sitting at home, feeling alone anymore. Success comes from your inner circle and community, from the connections and friendships you make. In business, I call these legacy business partnerships. But most of mine are friends also, because when you think about that Jim Rohn quote, "You are the average of the five people you spend the most time with," you must realize that's part of what's creating your dream life right now.

And it's not just those five people. It's the way they think about you, how they hold beliefs (energy) about you, and what you're capable of.

"People will rise or fall to the level of what their inner circle believes about them, whether those people verbalize that out loud or not."

That was an *aha* for me about "how" the five people idea works (or doesn't work).

To bring a big vision into reality, you need the right kind of people surrounding you.

"You need a vision big enough that other people want to help you build it."

I credit my friend Donnie Boivin for lighting a fire under me with that statement. It was the fuel for my vision of a community of holistic healers who help the world experience what's possible. When I reached out, offered to grab hands with my healer friends, and asked them to help me do that, they did. All of a sudden, it wasn't just me anymore; it was thousands of heart-centered, conscious, compassionate humans creating a bigger force together.

And my inner circle filled up with other visionaries. Now it was time to curate that circle at another level.

Visionaries see bigger pictures of what's possible. They thrive in collaboration and lead by creating amazing leaders within their communities. Most of my friends and colleagues are visionary, but I suspect they've never given themselves the time to sit and dream bigger. The prompts below will help you do that.

Let's Write

Remember to do your body and mind awareness practice (even if it's three breaths' worth) before you write. Set your timer for three minutes and write as fast as you can without censoring yourself. If three minutes isn't enough, give yourself as much time as needed and write until you're complete. You'll often notice a natural pause where the writing slows and finishes.

The Prompt

1. Your resources (money, time, people, energy) are limitless. What is your dream? Write as if it's happening now:

   I'm so happy and grateful now that _____.

2. What's the 10x version of the dream? Hint: Go even bigger and write as if it's happening now.

Room to write. . .

_____

_____

_____

_____

_____

_____

_____

_____

_____

_____

_____

_____

_____

_____

_____

_____

_____

_____

_____

_____

Feng Shui

This exercise will change your life and business. Decide which three to five people are the badasses who will get your time, energy, and attention in the form of true friendship this year. I'm not talking about talking on the phone once in a while or meeting for business chats on Zoom. I'm talking about taking-vacations-together friendship.

Reach out to one today with a fun note inviting them to chat!

Now you're writing your dream life into reality. You're living it on the page and as energy (in the form of feelings and emotions) in your body. This is the stuff of manifestation. The job now is to not get in the way of receiving what you're manifesting by letting doubt or fear interfere.

We'll go out with a couple more chapters about writing your dream life as a practice and sacred ritual.

Part 5

Write Your Dream Life Into Reality

The magic is in the ritual of love, gratitude, and joy that you make a part of your life every day, in every thought, word, and action, written or spoken. You're living it right now.

38.

The Discipline of Manifestation

Ever since I watched the movie, *The Secret,* something clicked, but then never fully worked. I became a powerful manifestor, and at the same time, I couldn't make it work *all* the time, or fast enough. Can you relate?

I had great breakthrough moments. There was the year I broke the multi-six-figure mark in my business, which taught me I wasn't limited to a six-figure salary. And closing $80k worth of business in one week was another huge breakthrough.

If I can close that many dollars of business in that short a time, I know (like really know) anything is possible, even much bigger amounts.

But I watched as doubt and fear invaded the sacred manifesting space in my mind. The conditioned what-ifs, energetic blocks, repetitive patterns, habits, and occurrences when it came to money—they tortured me. I trained myself to see them. But now I couldn't unsee them, and didn't have a solution. Until I began to turn all the things I learned into one big ritual, a lifestyle that served me in the highest and best ways.

My holistic healing journey taught me body and energy awareness, the most foundational key to all of this. My journaling and writing journey helped me become aware of negative thoughts and beliefs. My martial arts journey taught me to discipline my mind as I trained my physical body. My entrepreneurial journey helped me define purpose-driven fear and focus on my vision. My Law of Attraction research and practice gave me the science behind much of what I was doing. And my Feng Shui journey showed me how to curate my inner and outer spaces to match my dreams, goals, desires, and vision.

The magic lay in creating a daily living ritual that integrated all these powerful modalities.

Thinking positively will only get you part of the way there. "Ask, and it is given" will only serve you until you can't figure out how to receive. Pivoting and flipping the switch works for a while, until doubts and fears about the reality you're experiencing take over again and leave you where you started. Journaling what you're grateful for is a nice focus until you can't pay your next utility bill, and you end up using your journal as a garbage can for venting negativity.

I watched as my teachers all put a different spin on manifestation, recognizing each as an important piece of the puzzle. I created a way to write my dream life using a combination of body awareness, energy curation (inner and outer environments), ninja-level mindset, and journaling, all required to unlock the solution to consistent magic and manifestation.

I created a discipline of manifestation for my life. Now I understand that what's flowing to me is a direct result of my practice. Some weeks I'm on point. Other weeks, I falter. I'm human; my discipline is getting stronger and less wavering.

During my peak Taekwondo training, I competed in tournaments. I performed at my peak physically and mentally, and felt unstoppable. I trained three times a week and sometimes on my own at home. I committed myself to this level of mind-body fitness.

During my peak training moments in life, I didn't know if I'd make it through without breaking. It was a mental game. My anxiety was so high, I felt at my capacity both mentally and physically. I used breathwork and present-moment awareness and developed a level of patience and calm that serves me today, years after the trauma. My awareness game is on point, even beyond what it was as a third-degree black belt.

And now I get the game even more. We live the life we're living now.

You're living your dream life right now. Or not.

So whatever stage you're in, whatever you're going through, whatever good or bad thing is happening, or how you're feeling about it, your life is *now.*

Here's the question thread I use **when I'm not feeling good.** The last line (the writing) is where I set my timer for three minutes:

1. Do you notice the thoughts that don't serve you?

2. How do those thoughts make you feel?

3. Do you notice how those feelings don't serve you?

4. Is there anything you need to feel completely to honor any healing that needs to happen? If yes, do that. If no, continue.

5. Can you shift the thoughts to align with your goal state?

6. Can you shift the energy as you shift the thoughts and create a higher vibration? Think gratitude, love, or joy.

7. Remember your bigger vision, purpose, or desire and bring it to mind.

8. Write that down in detail. As you write, fully immerse yourself in the higher-vibration feelings. They're occurring in you right now, creating your reality.

When I'm feeling good and want to practice, I skip to #7 and #8. These last two steps are a regular part of my miracle morning, which includes walking and a cup of dark roast bulletproof butter coffee.

I write to Feng Shui my soul, so sometimes the writing comes out in a form that's in "lack" or "want." If that happens, I go up to #1 and shift it.

If the writing doesn't feel effective (I don't feel my vibes shift to a higher variety), I do some physical Feng Shui (clean, organize, or decorate my house, paying particular attention to the spaces I spend the most time in).

My writing ritual is daily.
My Feng Shui ritual is weekly.
My thought and feeling focus is hourly.

All these together create a discipline of manifestation.

Do you have a manifestation discipline?

You now have a chance to create your own "write your dream life" ritual or discipline. Include all the aspects that truly align and resonate with you, the practices that help you raise your vibe and live in joy and love. Your ritual or discipline might be different than mine. Take what you like from the chapters above, and add your own creative twists.

The power in your discipline of manifestation will be in the unique way you curate the thoughts, feelings, energy, and actions that best serve your dream life goals!

Let's Write

Remember to do your body and mind awareness practice (even if it's three breaths' worth) before you write. Set your timer for three minutes and write as fast as you can without censoring yourself. If three minutes isn't enough, give yourself as much time as needed and write until you're complete. You'll often notice a natural pause where the writing slows and finishes.

The Prompt

Create your own discipline or ritual of manifestation.

What practices will you include?

_____

_____

_____

When and how will you implement?

_____

_____

_____

How will you hold yourself accountable to your practice?

_____

_____

_____

Name three tools you can use on a tough day:

_____

_____

_____

Name three people you can reach out to on a tough day:

_____

_____

_____

In the last chapter, you'll have another chance to write your dream life into reality.

Feng Shui

Clean your whole house, room by room, remembering the tops of the curtains (start high and move to lower surfaces so dust shakes out from top to bottom), corners of the ceiling, and all the way down to the baseboards.

This may take a couple of days. Maybe it's time to hire a cleaning crew. Do what you need to do.

This is a never-ending practice. You'll get to the garage or the attic eventually. Take your time. As you clear, clean, and curate every space in your home, align with your biggest, best, juiciest, most joyful vision for your life. Enjoy!

39.

Write Your Dream Life

Here are a few final notes pages to inspire you to write your dream life.

What does the big dream look, feel, taste, sound, and smell like?

Write a vision so big that other people want to help you build it. And write like it's already happening:

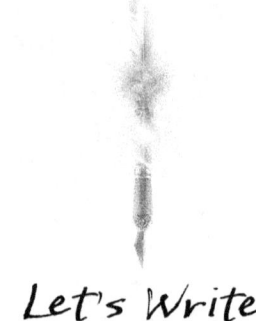

Let's Write

_____

_____

_____

_____

_____

_____

_____

_____

_____

_____

_____

_____

_____

_____

_____

_____

_____

About the Author

Laura Di Franco

Laura Di Franco is the CEO of Brave Healer Productions (including Brave Business Books and Brave Kids Books), an award-winning publisher for holistic health, wellness, and business professionals who want to become bestselling authors, build their community and business, and leave their legacy in a more conscious way.

She holds a master's degree and 30 years of experience in holistic physical therapy, is a third-degree black belt in Taekwondo, and is the author of 15 books. Brave Healer Productions has published over 100 Amazon bestselling books with a mission to help the world experience what's possible.

Laura is a divorced mom (of two adult kids and one dog), lover of sunrises and dark chocolate, spoken-word poet, inspirational speaker, and is convinced she was a race car driver in a past life. She has a contagious passion for helping you share brave words that build your business and leave your legacy.

Come Write with Us!

Get access to The Brave Healer Resources Vault with thousands of dollars worth of training, master classes, and workshops for author-entrepreneurs: https://lauradifranco.com/resources-vault/

Want to write in our next expert book collaboration?

Find our projects here:
https://lauradifranco.com/expert-book-collaborations/

Connect with Laura:

Website: https://BraveHealer.com

LinkedIn: https://www.linkedin.com/in/thelauradifranco/

YouTube:
https://www.youtube.com/c/BraveHealerProductionswithLauraDiFranco

A Special Note of Thanks

"Laura, whatcha writing this year?"

I looked up from across the wooden cafe table at my BFF. The last time we lunched was at least a year ago.

Maybe two, I thought.

"I'm almost done with *Write Your Dream Life,*" I said. "I started writing it last year when I pulled out a dusty bin of journals from under my bed and realized I had decades' worth of venting clogging up my energy."

"What? Whoa! Tell me more."

"Well, over my many years of learning about Law of Attraction, healing, energy, and all those fun things, I've learned from so many great teachers. But they all seem to give us only one piece of the puzzle.

"I did a really cool Feng Shui certification this year, and my teacher was integrating the writing with some of her Feng Shui techniques. My lightbulb went off.

"Nobody has put together the writing, with the positive thinking and mindset practice, with the Feng Shui, with the energetic principles. So, *Write Your Dream Life* is a book with stories about awareness and the practical application of all these things."

"That sounds fabulous."

I watched her face as she replied and noticed her familiar, genuine smile and enthusiasm. *This woman has always believed in me more than I have.*

"When is it out?" she asked.

"Sometime in the first quarter of 2026, I think. I'm still finishing up the writing."

"Awesome, let me know, and I'll buy one for all my friends."

She grabbed her cappuccino and sipped, pulling a small leather notebook out of her purse. She always made a list of things we needed to talk about.

Dear Shelly, you were the origin story of my belief that I could do everything I dreamed of. Thank you. I love you.

Rampage of Gratitude

To the community of Brave Healers who continually show up to light my fire of purpose and vision—how lucky I am to play in the sandbox with you all every day! I love you. Thank you for being in my world.

To Dana Claudat, thank you for shining your light in the world and for your generous teachings that have brought me to another level of living my dream life. These teachings have created profound shifts for me and so many others. I love you. Thank you for everything you do.

To my teachers, masters, coaches, and mentors, so many of you who provided your life mastery to your students and communities, thank you for your work and for the care and attention you gave to your students. Thank you, Master John L. Holloway, John F. Barnes, John Upledger, Esther Hicks, Torrie Pattillo, Steve Harrison, Jack Canfield, Laura Munson, Marie Forleo, Jon Morrow, Amy Birks, Holly Jackson, Honorée Corder, Katie Nelson, Justin Breen, Randy Molland, and Brandon Fong. There are so many others in a lifetime of learning, y'all!

To Kelly vdH - Kaschula, the cover and interior designer of *Write Your Dream Life,* and Director of Brave Kids Books, thank you for your steadfast support, enthusiasm, and love, and for manifesting the vision alongside me.

To Haley Walden, my editor. Finding you was a small miracle. The Universe had my back when I asked for an editor who "got it." I'm so grateful for you.

To our book launch team, thank you for showing up to read, purchase, and review. Thank you for your interest, time, enthusiasm, and your generous kind words about the book. You are the face of our purpose every single day.

I write to Feng Shui my soul, to clear a space inside, connect to my inner wisdom, and inspire you to be brave and live your dream life.

Come play with me and others who are staying accountable to a higher-vibe, world-changing kind of life.

You'll find the **Write Your Dream Life Community & Manifestation Club** at:

https://writeyourdreamlife.com/

With Warrior Love,

Laura